1 MONTH OF
FREE
READING

at

www.ForgottenBooks.com

By purchasing this book you are eligible for one month membership to ForgottenBooks.com, giving you unlimited access to our entire collection of over 1,000,000 titles via our web site and mobile apps.

To claim your free month visit:
www.forgottenbooks.com/free720183

ISBN 978-0-484-59928-3
PIBN 10720183

THIRD ANNUAL REPORT

OF THE

HORTICULTURAL SOCIETY

AND

Fruit Growers' Association

OF

BRITISH COLUMBIA

WITH

PEST AND REMEDY

SUPPLEMENT

1892

VANCOUVER, B. C.

PRINTED AT THE NEWS-ADVERTISER PRINTING AND BOOKBINDING ESTABLISHMENT
CAMBIE STREET

THIRD ANNUAL REPORT

OF THE

HORTICULTURAL SOCIETY

AND

Fruit Growers' Association

OF

BRITISH COLUMBIA

WITH

PEST AND REMEDY

SUPPLEMENT

1892

VANCOUVER, B. C.

PRINTED AT THE NEWS-ADVERTISER PRINTING AND BOOKBINDING ESTABLISHMENT

CAMBIE STREET

First Officers

J. M. BROWNING - - - - - - - President
THOS. CUNNINGHAM - - - - - Vice-President
G. W. HENRY - - - - - - Second Vice-President
A. H. B. MACGOWAN, Secretary-Treasurer.

Officers for 1890

W. J. HARRIS - - - - - - - President
O. D. SWEET - - - - - First Vice-President
A. C. WELLS - - - - - - Second Vice-President
A. H. B. MACGOWAN, Secretary-Treasurer.

Officers for 1891

W. J. HARRIS - - - - - - - President
JOHN KIRKLAND - - - - First Vice-President
O. D. SWEET - - - - - - Second Vice-President
A. H. B. MACGOWAN, Secretary-Treasurer.

Officers for 1892

W. J. HARRIS - - - - - - - President
THOS. CUNNINGHAM - - - - First Vice-President
N. BUTCHART - - - - - - Second Vice-President
A. H. B. MACGOWAN, Secretary-Treasurer.

Directors for 1892

Agassiz, GEORGE A. BEEBE
"   T. A. SHARP
Ashcroft, EX-GOVERNOR CORNWALL
Burton Prairie, H. P. BALES
Cache Creek, C. A. SEMLIN, M.P.P.
Chilliwhack, I. KIPP
"   A. C. WELLS
"   J. H. BENT
Comox, J. A. HALIDAY
Cowichan, J. BRADWELL
Donald, A. W. MANUEL
Esquimalt, HON. C. E. POOLEY
Hatzic, R. L. CODD
Hammond, G. W. HENRY
Harrison River, T. WILSON
Howe Sound, GEO. GIBSON
Kamloops, H. McCUTCHEON
"   J. A. MARA
Ladner's Landing, E. HUTCHERSON
"   "   J. KIRKLAND
"   "   W. H. LADNER
Langley, JOHN MAXWELL

Langley, JAS. McADAM
Lillooet, C. A. PHAIR
Luln Island, J. RUPERT FOSTER
Maple Ridge, W. J. HARRIS
"   JOHN WHITE
Matsqui, C. B. SWORD
"   H. F. PAGE
Mission City, F. S. TIMBERLAKE
Mayne Island, T. R. FIGG
Nicola, JOHN CLAPERTON
North Arm, W. J. BRANDRITH
New Westminster,
"   PETER LATHAM
"   THOS. CUNNINGHAM
"   A. C. WILSON
"   T. R. PEARSON
"   MARSHALL SINCLAIR
Okanagan, ALFRED POSTILL
"   GEO. WHELAN
"   LORD ABERDEEN
"   HON. MAJORIBANKS
Pender Island, W. GRIMMER

DIRECTORS FOR 1892—(CONTINUED)

Port Haney, HECTOR FERGUSON

Port Moody, NORVAL BUTCHART

Richmond, O. D. SWEET

Saanich, J. D. BRYANT

Salt Spring Island,

          J. P. BOOTH, M.P.P.

Spallumcheen, DONALD GRAHAM

Spence's Bridge, JOHN MURRAY

Squamish, E. B. MADILL

Sumas, ALLEN EVANS

Surrey, J. PUNCH, M.P.P.

Vancouver, J. M. BROWNING

Vancouver, G. G. McKAY

    "   R. E. GOSNELL

    "   R. T. ROBINSON

    "   WALTER TAYLOR

    "   A. H. B. MACGOWAN

Victoria, G. A. McTAVISH

    "   D. W. HIGGINS

    "   MR. JAY

    "   D. KER

    "   C. E. RENOUF

    "   W. H. BAINBRIDCE

HONORARY MEMBERS

OF THE

HORTICULTURAL SOCIETY AND FRUIT GROWERS' ASSOCIATION OF

BRITISH COLUMBIA

HON. HUGH NELSON   HON. JOHN ROBSON

HON. F. G. VERNON   HON. J. H. TURNER   HON. THEO. DAVIE

DAVID OPPENHEIMER, ESQUIRE

LIST OF MEMBERS

of the

HORTICULTURAL SOCIETY AND FRUIT GROWERS' ASSOCIATION OF

BRITISH COLUMBIA

ALLEN, N., Vancouver
ANDERSON, V. F., New Westminster
ARMSTRONG, R. G., New Westminster
ARTHUR, WM., Ladners
AUSTIN, W. R., New Westminster
BROWNING, J. M., Vancouver
BRANDRITH, W. J., Vancouver
BALES, H. P., Burton Prairie
BODWELL, E. V., Vancouver
BOULTBEE, J., Vancouver
BRYANT, J. D., Saanich
BEST, JAS., Port Haney
BECKET, W. R., Port Haney
BUTCHART, J., Moodyville
BLACKBURN, J., Vancouver
BLACKSTOCK, ROBT., Hammond
BOSOMWORTH, T., Port Haney
BRADFORD, F. F., Revelstoke
BRYMNER, G. D., New Westminster
BONSON, L. F., New Westminster
BENNET, F., Mayne Island
BENT, J. H., Vancouver
BOOTH, J. P., Salt Spring Island
BROADWELL, —., Salt Spring Island
BERROW, A. A., Salt Spring Island
BAINBRIDGE, W. H., Victoria
BROWN, WM., Victoria
BROWNLEY, J. H., Victoria
BRENTON, J., Vancouver
BEDDOES, S. J., Vesuvius Bay
CUNNINGHAM, T., New Westminster
CANNING, J., Vancouver
CLARKE, CHAS., Vancouver
COTTON. F.-C., Vancouver
CARGILL, WM., Vancouver
CLARK, R., Vancouver
CLAPPERTON, J., Nicola
CLARK, T. W., Vancouver
CLIFTON, CHAS., Matsqui
CAMPBELL, A. O., New Westminster

CUNNINGHAM, H. M., New West'r
CURTIS, D. S., New Westminster
CORNWALL, C. F., Ashcroft
CROFT, HY., Victoria
CURRIE, J. P., Upper Sumas
CORDINER, P., Vancouver
COX, WM., Clover Point
C. CLAWSON, New Westminster
DUNN, THOS., Vancouver
DOCKLEADER, D., Port Haney
DANIELS, WM., Vancouver
DALLEY, EDWIN, Nicola
DALLEY, WM., Victoria
DODDS, WM., Victoria
McDONALD & McGILL, New Whatcom
ELDON, GEO., Vancouver
EWAN, A., New Westminster
FAY, REV. P., Vancouver
FEWSTER, PHILIP, Vancouver
FIGG, T. R., Mayne Island
FERGUSON, H., Port Haney
FOSTER, J. P., Vancouver
FISHER, J. B., New Westminster
FALES, W. E., New Westminster
FALDING, W. H., New Westminster
GOSNELL, R. E., Vancouver
GAMBLE, A. G., New Westminsier
GRANT, G. D., New Westminster
GARDINER, R. C., Johnston's Land'g
HERBERT, B. W., Vancouver
HUTCHERSON, E., Ladner's
HOWELL, ALEX., Vancouver
HARRIS, W. J., Maple Ridge
HENRY, G. W., Port Hammond
HALPENNY, J. G., Nanaimo
HANEY, T., Port Haney
HENDERSON, J. C., Chilliwhack
HAMMOND, J., Port Hammond
HALL, Z. S., New Westminster
HICKS, H. A., Ladner's

HENRY, M. H., Vancouver
HUFF, G. A., Saywarl, Alberni
HENLEY, H., Clover Point
HARRIS, Mrs. D. R., Victoria
JOHNSTON, M. T., Victoria
JOHNSTON, W., New Westminster
INGLIS, R. S., Port Moody
KENNEDY, G., New Westminster
KENNEDY, J. M., New Westminster
KIPP, ISAAC, Chilliwhack
KERR, D. R., Victoria
LAWSON, J. W., Vancouver
LAITY, J., Port Hammond
LADNER, W. H., Ladner's
LATHAM, P., New Westminster
LAW, R., New Westminster
MAY, W. H., Vancouver
MURRAY, JOHN, Spence's Bridge
MURRAY, R., Port Hammond
MILLER, J., Vancouver
MERRILL, T. M., Vancouver
MARTIN, O., Port Haney
MACGOWAN, A. H. B., Vancouver
MAJOR, C. G., New Westminster
MOWAT, MAX, New Westminster
MEAD, GEO., New Westminster
MAWDSLEY, W. H., Mayne Island
MARA, J. A., Kamloops
MOSS, JAS., Victoria
McCOLL, WM., New Westminster
McDONALD, B. C., New Westminster
McDONALD & McGILL, N. W'tc'm,W.
McFADDEN, —., New Westminster
McGILLIVRAY, WM., Vancouver
McGILLIVRAY, D., Sumas
McGREGOR, P. C., Victoria
McKAY, G. G., Vancouver
McKAMING, R. C., Popcum
McKEON, W. J., Victoria
McLAGAN, J. C., Vancouver
McLEAN, A., New Westminster
McMILLAN, W. J., Vancouver
McNEELY, THOS., Ladner's
McPHERSON, R. G., New West'r
McRAE, D., Vancouver
McTAVISH, G. A., Vancouver

NEWTON, W. G., Port Hammond
NELSON, W., Port Hammond
OGLE, E. W., New Westminster
OHLSON, ANDREW, Victoria
PROUT, W., Victoria
PUNCH, J., Surrey
POWIS, J., Vancouver
POSTILL, A., Okanagan
PEARSON, T. R., New Westminster
PORT. E. H., New Westminster
PHILLIPS, JAS., New Westminster
PHILLIPS, E. S., Vancouver
PAGE, H. F., Matsqui
POOLEY, WM., Nicola
PATTERSON, MISS J. A., New West'r
ROBERTSON, S., Langley
ROBERTSON, D. Agassiz
RAND, C. D., Vancouver
ROBINSON, R. T., Vancouver
ROWLING, W. H., Vancouver
RAND, A., New Westminster
ROBERTSON, C. J., New Westminster
ROSS, M., New Westminster
READ, H. T., New Westminster
RAYMOND, G., New Westminster
RAE, G. D., New Westminster
RITCHIE, A., Warnock
RENOUF, C. E., Victoria
SWEET, O. D., Richmond
SINCLAIR, C., Cache Creek
SALSBURY, W. F., Vancouver
SINCLAIR, J. W., Port Hammond
STEPHENS, J., Port Haney
SINCLAIR, J. F., Port Haney
SPINKS, J. M., Vancouver
SUTHERLAND, M., Vancouver
SHARP, T. A., Agassiz
SINCLAIR, M., New Westminster
SHADWELL, H. B., New Westminster
SMITH, E. A., Vancouver
STEWART, R. F., Vancouver
SMALL, G., New Westminster
SHAKESPEARE, N., Victoria
SPROAT, JOHN, New Westminster
SCOTT, W. E., Salt Spring Island
TOWNLEY, C. R., Vancouver

TOWNLEY, J. D., Vancouver
THOMAS, JOHN, Port Haney
TEITJEN, WM., New Westminster
TRAPP, T. J., New Westminster
TIDY, S. G., New Westminster
TAIT, REV. C. M., Chilliwhack
TURNER, WM., Vancouver
VOWELL, A. W., Donald
WALWORTH, J. L., Vancouver
WHITE, J. W., Port Hammond
WEBBER, D. C., Port Hammond
WILSON, A., Vancouver
WILSON, J. J., Maple Ridge
WINTEMUTE, B., Vancouver

WOLFENDEN, G., New Westminster
WALKER, W. J., New Westminster
WALKER, ----, New Westminster
WOODS, C. E., New Westminster
WILSON, A. C., New Westminster
WELLS, A. C., Chilliwhack
WEBB, H., Chilliwhack
WILSON, TOM, Harrison River
WALDEN, W., Warnock
CHAS. WARRICK, New Westminster
WILKINSON, J. I., Chilliwhack
WENNET, J. W., Victoria
WARLOCK, F. A., Victoria

HORTICULTURAL · SOCIETY

-----AND-----

FRUIT GROWERS' ASSOCIATION

In January, 1891, the following circular was sent out to members and others :

British Columbia Horticultural Society and Fruit Growers' Association.

VANCOUVER, B. C., January, 1891.

DEAR SIR,

Agreeable with a resolution passed at annual meeting, I am sending each director some membership tickets. They are sent with a view of securing new members. Directors are requested to dispose of all they can at $2.00 each, after filling in blanks, and writing his (director's) name across the card, sending me name and post office address of each person who takes a ticket.

Any member desiring raspberries of the following kinds will receive same by notifying Mr. G. W. Henry, Hammond, who has offered to distribute free in following quantities, viz. : half a dozen "Golden Queen," or one dozen "Cuthbert" or "Marlborough."

Mr. E. Hutcherson, Ladner's Landing, will, during the coming season, forward to members one "Box ELDER" or "Ash Leaf Maple," a hardy ornamental lawn tree. Those who received the WHITE ASH FRAXINES and CATALPLEA SPECIOSA, distributed by Mr. Hutcherson last season, will oblige by reporting what success they had with same.

If members desiring to have questions answered on Fruit Growing or Horticulture will forward their questions to the secretary, he will endeavor to have correct answers given through the press or by letter.

The association is arranging for the publication in a British Columbia newspaper of original matter and extracts from other papers, pamphlets, etc., treating on FRUIT GROWING, HORTICULTURE and AGRICULTURE. Members are particularly requested to forward to the secretary such original matter as they may feel disposed ; also, any interesting cuttings they may be in a position to secure. It is expected to use one or two columns of the paper, and it being desirable to make this a most interesting part of our work, each member is expected to be a contributor.

The benefits of the association are being felt by members and others. The good work that is being done is appreciated, and it is realized that there is much room for expansion.

ALL MEMBERS are requested to remit amount of dues promptly, and, if possible, accompany same with names and entrance fees for some new members.

The *Canadian Horticulturist* will be ordered for each member who pays subscription for 1891.

Yours respectfully,

A. H. B. MACGOWAN,

Secretary.

LADNER'S LANDING, May 5th, 1891.

The quarterly meeting of the directors of the Horticultural Society and Fruit Growers' Association was held in the town hall at 5.45 p.m., the vice-president, Mr. John Kirkland, in the chair, and Mr. A. H. B. Macgowan, secretary of the association, officiated in that capacity.

The following gentlemen were also present : Messrs. John Lister, Thos. Cunningham, T. R. Pearson, Peter Latham and D. J. Munn, of Westminster; D. McGillivray, Sumas; N. Butchart, Port Moody; R. T. Robinson, Vancouver; D. L. Lockerby, Montreal; J. T. Wilkinson, Chilliwack; W. Knight, Popcum; Mr. Bush, Harrison River; Thos. McNeely, W. H. Ladner and E. Hutcherson, of Ladners, and representatives of *The Columbian, News-Advertiser* and *World.*

The vice-president regretted that president Harris was unable to be present, owing to illness in his family. He felt a deep interest in the society, and had great pleasure in welcoming the members to Ladners.

The reading of the minutes of the last meeting was dispensed with, and the minutes adopted.

COMMUNICATIONS.

The secretary, Mr. Macgowan, said that in answer to inquiries as to the growth of catalpa and ash, distributed last spring, there was only one response, from Plumpers Pass, but that was very satisfactory. He also read a communication from England, making inquiries as to fruit growing, by an intending settler.

There was also a letter from the Vancouver *World*, offering a column of space to the association in the weekly edition. The secretary had called for original matter from the members to fill it, but it had not been taken advantage of to any great extent. He urged upon the directors that they should send original contributions to this column, and good clippings.

From Mr. Kerr, Victoria, in regard to holding a meeting at Nanaimo or Victoria.

From the Lieut-Governor, acknowledging receipt of the association's letter asking for a larger grant.

Mr. Macgowan remarked that the grant had been increased to $1,000 this year.

The secretary read a telegram from Mr. Henry, saying it was impossible for him to attend the meeting.

The secretary remarked that at the close of the annual meeting he called for tenders for printing the annual report, but the report was not yet ready. He hoped it would soon be out. He had ordered 2,000 copies. *Telegram* Printing Co. being lowest, they had been given the contract.

Moved by Thos. Cunningham, seconded by E. Hutcherson, and resolved, That the thanks of this meeting be tendered to the Provincial Government for the liberal grant of $1,000 for the purpose of this society, and that the secretary be instructed to forward this resolution to Hon. John Robson.

Mr. Hutcherson presented the following address to the association, from the Delta Agricultural Society ;

GENTLEMEN,—This occasion of your visit to Ladners, and holding one of your interesting meetings affords an opportunity that is most gladly seized by the members of the Delta Agricultural Society to convey to you a most cordial and fraternal welcome to our Delta lands.

The benefits derived from the work of your association are apparent even to those who are not fruit growers, and the country in general profits very much by your work.

Your object, I believe, is to disseminate such information as will assist persons in every part of this province to select the best varieties of fruit adapted to their several localities, and thus prevent many failures and save valuable time. You thus encourage and increase the growing of fruit and add to the commerce of the country. This district and all the districts from which you have come are capable of almost indefinite extension in fruit growing, and the greater the extension within reasonable limits, the greater will be the benefits to this country. In addition to the commercial benefits that arise, is the great benefit which results to the health of the people from the use of fruit as a diet.

I again bid you welcome to the Delta, and am confident that your treatment here will be such that you will go away feeling that Ladners is at least not the most forsaken place in the world.

E. HUTCHERSON,

President.

Mr. Thos. Cunningham moved, seconded by T. R. Pearson, that this meeting cordially reciprocate the kind expressions of welcome from the Delta Agricultural Society, and express the hope that our meeting will be mutually beneficial. Carried.

Mr. E. Hutcherson moved, seconded by Mr. Thos. Cunningham, that the annual show be held in Victoria.

Mr. Cunningham said the society should extend its operations all over the province. He had made enquiries in Victoria as to the amount of fruit grown there, and was surprised to find such extensive orchards. He had had repeated enquiries as to how to become members of the association, and he would suggest that the secretary could possibly double the membership by properly canvassing the Island.

Mr. John Lister said that Vancouver was more of a supporter of the association than Westminster.

Mr. Cunningham said the list at present showed very well for Westminster, and he could not sit still and hear strictures on that city.

Mr. E. Hutcherson said wherever the show was held the membership increased on account of it. He thought at present Westminster was ahead of Vancouver in membership.

Mr. W. H. Ladner said the representatives of the society came from all parts of the Mainland, but none from the Island. He hoped to see it grow into an important industry, but it was not right for the Island to ask the society to hold its meetings there when it did not send a single representative here.

Mr. Peter Latham thought that Vancouver should have the exhibition. They had a double grant this year, and something should be done in connection with representing the Fruit Association well in the Agricultural Exhibition in Westminster.

Mr. Hutcherson said that Mr. McTavish, of Victoria, had done more than any single man at the exhibition last year.

Mr. Thos. Cunningham said every member from the Island had supported the Government grant. Every inducement should be offered Victoria to stop the importation of fruit from the Sound.

Mr. Kirkland said the grant was from the whole province. It would be no reflection on Vancouver if it went to Victoria this year. They should cultivate a friendly spirit with all parts of the province.

Mr. Hutcherson said his reason for the exhibition going to Victoria was to increase the scope of the society.

Mr. R. T. Robinson, of Vancouver, said that the Island should have its turn, and he thought the exhibition this year should be held on the Island.

Mr. Macgowan said that previous to the last exhibition, Westminster had only five or six members, but many had subscribed handsomely then to the exhibition, and had been placed on the list as members. He believed the benefits of the association should be widespread, and it would make a better feeling between the Island and the Mainland to hold the exhibition in Victoria.

The motion was then carried.

Moved by Mr. Cunningham, seconded by Mr. Pearson, Resolved that the following be appointed a special committee for local arrangement of exhibition matter : Mayor Grant, Alderman Renouf, John Kirkland, G. A. McTavish, Wm. Dalbey, D. B. Kerr, Hy. Croft and Noah Shakespeare.

Moved by Mr. Cunningham, seconded by Mr. Hutcherson, Resolved that Messrs. Hutcherson, Henry, Latham and the secretary be a committee to fix date of holding exhibition at Victoria.

Moved by Mr. Hutcherson, seconded by Mr. Pearson, Resolved that Messrs. Cunningham, Robinson, Henry and Hutcherson be a committee to revise prize lists.

Moved by Mr. Cunningham, seconded by Mr. Robinson, Resolved that, at request of directors of Royal Exhibition and Industrial Association, this association take charge of the fruit, flower and vegetable department of show at New Westminster.

NEW WESTMINSTER, July 3rd, 1891.—Meeting of committee of British Columbia Horticultural Society and Fruit Growers' Association.—Present, Thos. Cunningham (chairman), G. W. Henry, E. Hutcherson, P. Latham and A. H. B. Macgowan.

Moved by Mr. Hutcherson, seconded by Mr. Henry, Resolved that exhibition be held at Victoria on Tuesday and Wednesday, 11th and 12th August.

Prize list was read and passed, allowing—

Class A	$ 133.00
Class B	164.50
Class C	255.00
Class D	165.50
	$ 718.00

Moved by Mr. Henry, seconded by Mr. Latham, Resolved that this committee appoint a judge in each class, and request local committee to appoint another, the following being appointed by this committee : Peter Latham, classes A and B ; A. W. Wright, class C ; John King, class D.

VICTORIA, B. C., August 12th, 1891.--Meeting of directors of the Horticultural Society and Fruit Growers' Association of British Columbia.— Present, John Kirkland, (vice-president) in chair ; E. Hutcherson, Ladners ; John Lister, New Westminster ; G. A. McTavish, city ; Peter Latham, New Westminster : G. W. Henry, Port Hammond ; Wm. Knight, Popcum ; W. H. Bainbridge. Hy. Croft, city ; W. Hicks, Wm. Arthur, Ladner's ; A. H. B. Macgowan.

Minutes of May 5th, 1891, were read and, on motion, confirmed.

Mr. Bainbridge, secretary of exhibition committee, presented minutes of said committee, which were read and received.

Moved by Mr. Hutcherson, seconded by Mr. Henry, Resolved that this association assume the responsibility of paying the prize list.

Moved by Mr. Henry, seconded by Mr. Latham, That Messrs. G. A. McTavish. E. Hutcherson, G. W. Henry, Mr. Latham and the secretary be a committee to prepare a system of questions to be circulated throughout the province.

Mr. Hutcherson, from committee on management of New Westminster show, reported that professional gardeners were refusing to exhibit at New Westminster on account of smallness of prizes and arrangement of prize list.

Moved by Mr. McTavish, seconded by Mr. Macgowan, Resolved that this meeting endorse the action of the committee in preparing the prize list for New Westminster show.

Moved by Mr. Hutcherson, seconded by Mr. McTavish, Resolved that the secretary's salary be $30 per month for current year.

Moved by Mr. McTavish, seconded by Mr. Latham, Resolved that travelling expenses, including hotel bills, of all special committees be paid by the association.

Moved by Mr. Hutcherson, seconded by Mr. Henry, Resolved that Messrs. G. A. McTavish, Wm. Knight, Wm. Arthur, P. Latham, G. W. Henry, J. Lister, E. Hutcherson be a committee to arrange matters in connection with exhibition at New Westminster.

The following were suggested as such committees :

On Fruit.—Messrs. Hutcherson, Henry and Knight.
On Flowers.—Messrs. McTavish and Latham.
On Vegetables.—Messrs. Arthur and Lister.

The following judges were appointed :

On Vegetables.—Messrs. J. Lister and John King.
On Flowers.—Messrs. Geo. Jay, senr., and Peter Latham.
On Fruit.—Messrs. R. V. Winch and J. Clearihue.

Moved by Mr. McTavish, seconded by Mr. Hutcherson, Resolved that next meeting of directors be held at New Westminster, at 10 o'clock a.m., on 24th September.

Moved by Mr. Hutcherson, seconded by Mr. McTavish, Resolved that the secretary be instructed to write Mr. Joel Broadwell, Salt Spring Island, for history of seedling apple (presented for naming) and habits of tree, whether strong grower, heavy bearer, or early ripener, etc.

Moved by Mr. Henry, seconded by Mr. Latham, Resolved that the thanks of the association be presented to the committee on local management of the exhibition, and, through them to the C.P.N. Co. for reduced fares and courtesies received.

Meeting adjourned.

***

The annual exhibition was held at Victoria on August 11th and 12th, 1892. From the *Times'* report is clipped the following:

At the Assembly Hall this afternoon there was noticeable a great improvement in the rich display of flowers and plants of yesterday, a number of ladies and gentlemen having sent in this morning, simply for the purpose of adding to the attractiveness of the show, a choice variety of most beautiful flowers. Among those deserving of praise, and to whom the directors of the show feel under deep obligation for the special interest displayed are: Mr. Jas. Moss, who brought in a number of the choicest hollyhocks ever seen in the province, and who has worked like a Trojan all day in adding to the decorations; Lady Nelson, who went to considerable expense and vast trouble in bringing to the exhibition the choicest flowers of the Government House conservatory; Mrs. R. D. Harris, who kindly supplied some beautiful plants, and Mr. McTavish, who also helped largely to make the show a success, by exhibiting rare flowers. Mr. Hasenfratz to-day brought a fuschia and geranium that for beauty and size would defy the best professional gardeners to beat. The exhibition, in so far as the class of flowers shown goes, is a grand success, but there is no doubt that if more interest had been taken by the many amateurs of the city, whose lovely gardens are to be seen on every side, Victoria would have made such a display as would vie with the best in Canada. The attendance last night and to-day has been fair, and there is no doubt that this evening the ball will be crowded   This is the last day of the exhibition, and all who fail to visit the place this evening will miss seeing the most gorgeous display of flowers ever shown in Victoria.

Following is the prize list :

CLASS A.

Collection of decorative and flowering plants, not less than 15 or more than 24—1st ($5), G. A. McTavish, Victoria; 2nd ($3), W. Brown, Victoria.

Collection of decorative and flowering plants, for amateurs only—1st ($4), D. R. Harris, Victoria.

Tuberous Begonias, single, 6 plants—1st ($2), W. Brown, Victoria; 2nd ($1.50), G. A. McTavish, Victoria.

Tuberous Begonias, double, 4 plants—1st ($2), W. Brown, Victoria; 2nd ($1.50), G. A. McTavish, Victoria.

Begonias, 4, in bloom—1st ($1.50), G. A. McTavish, Victoria; 2nd ($1), D. R. Harris, Victoria.

Begonias, Rex, in bloom—1st ($1.50), W. Brown, Victoria; 2nd ($1), G. A. McTavish, Victoria.

Coleus, in bloom—1st ($1.50), W. Brown, Victoria.

Foliage plants, in bloom—1st ($2.50), G. A. McTavish, Victoria; 2nd ($1.50), W. Brown, Victoria.

Fern plants—1st ($2.50) W. Brown, Victoria.

Fern plants—1st ($2.50), G. A. McTavish, Victoria.

Collection of palms—1st ($3), G. A. McTavish, Victoria.

Fuschias, 3, in bloom—1st ($3), G. A. McTavish, Victoria.

Fuschias, 1, in bloom—1st ($2), G. A. McTavish, Victoria.

Geraniums—1st ($3), G. A. McTavish, Victoria.

Gloxinias—1st ($3), W. Brown, Victoria.

Hanging basket—1st ($3), G. A. McTavish, Victoria.

Heliotrope—1st ($1.50), G. A. McTavish, Victoria.

Pelargoniums—1st ($1.50), G. A. McTavish, Victoria.

Tuberoses—1st ($1.50), G. A. McTavish, Victoria,

Best plant—1st ($3), G. A. McTavish, Victoria.

Collection of ferns—1st ($2), J. R. Anderson, Victoria.

Cactus—1st ($2), G. A. McTavish, Victoria.

Annuals, collection—1st ($3), G. A. McTavish, Victoria; 2nd ($2), G. W. Henry, Port Hammond.

Asters, collection—1st ($1.50), W. Dodds, Victoria; 2nd ($1), G. A. McTavish, Victoria; 3rd (50c.), G. W. Henry, Port Hammond.

Bouquet, hand—1st ($2), G. A. McTavish, Victoria ; 2nd ($1.50), S. G. Tidy, Westminster ; 3rd ($1), W. Dodds, Victoria.

Bouquet, table—1st ($2), Jas. Moss, Victoria.

Cut flowers, basket—1st ($2), G. A. McTavish, Victoria ; 2nd ($1.50), S. G. Tidy, Westminster ; 3rd ($1), G. W. Henry, Port Hammond.

Cut flowers, collection—1st ($5), D. R. Harris, Victoria ; 2nd ($3), G. A. McTavish, Victoria.

Dahlias, Double—1st ($2), G. W. Henry, Port Hammond ; 2nd ($1.50), Jas. Moss, Victoria.

Dahlias, single—1st ($2), Jas. Moss, Victoria.

Dahlias, Dwarf Pompon—1st ($2), G. W. Henry, Port Hammond.

Dahlias, cactus—1st ($2), G. W. Henry, Port Hammond.

Gladioli—1st ($3), Jas. Moss, Victoria ; 2nd ($2), W. Dodds, Victoria ; 3rd ($1), G. A. McTavish, Victoria.

Pansies—1st ($2), Geo. Millett, Victoria ; 2nd ($1), G. A. McTavish, Victoria ; 3rd (50c), G. W. Henry, Port Hammond.

Petunias, double—1st ($2), G. A. McTavish, Victoria : 2nd ($1), W. Dodds, Victoria.

Petunias, single—1st ($2), G. A. McTavish, Victoria.

Phlox Drummondii—1st ($2), G. W. Henry, Port Hammond ; 2nd ($1), G. A. McTavish, Victoria ; 3rd (50c.), Jas. Moss, Victoria.

Phlox Perennial—1st ($2), Jas. Moss, Victoria ; 2nd ($1), G. W. Henry, Port Hammond.

Carnations—1st ($2), Jas. Moss, Victoria ; 2nd ($1), G. A. McTavish, Victoria.

Verbenas—1st ($2), D. R. Harris, Victoria ; 2nd ($1), G. W. Henry, Port Hammond.

Stocks—1st ($2), W. Dodds, Victoria ; 2nd ($1), G. A. McTavish, Victoria ; 3rd (50c.), D. R. Harris, Victoria.

Zinnias—1st ($2), W. Brown, Victoria.

Everlastings—1st ($2), H. N. Rich, Ladners.

Lilies—1st ($2), G. A. McTavish, Victoria.

Roses Hybrid, Perpetual—2nd ($3), G. W. Henry, Port Hammond.

Roses Hybrid, Crimson—1st ($2), G. A. McTavish, Victoria.

Roses Hybrid, Pink—1st ($2), G. A. McTavish, Victoria.

Roses, Tea—2nd ($2), G. A. McTavish, Victoria ; 3rd ($1), G. W. Henry, Port Hammond.

Floral design—1st ($3), G. A. McTavish, Victoria ; 2nd ($2), S. G. Tidy, Westminster ; 3rd ($1), W. Brown, Victoria.

Bridal Bouquet—1st ($3), W. Dodds, Victoria ; 2nd ($2), G. A. McTavish, Victoria ; 3rd ($1), S. G. Tidy, Westminster.

Funeral Design—1st ($3), G. A. McTavish, Victoria ; 2nd ($2), W. Brown, Victoria.

Apples, yellow transparent—1st ($3), W. Arthur, Ladners; 2nd ($2), Jubilee Farm, Ladners.

Apples, Red Astrachan—1st ($3), J. Whitfield, Victoria ; 2nd ($2), Jubilee Farm, Ladners ; 3rd ($1), T. McNeely, Ladners.

Apples, Duchess of Oldenburg—1st ($3), Jubilee Farm, Ladners.

Apples, Gravenstein—1st ($3), Jubilee Farm, Ladners.

Apples, Tetofsky—1st ($3), W. Beaumont, Maple Bay.

Apples, any other summer apple—1st ($3), W. Arthur, Ladners.

Apples, Crab—1st ($3), W. Knight, Popcum ; 2nd ($2), W. Arthur, Ladners ; 3rd ($1), Jubilee Farm, Ladners.

Pears, Madeline—1st ($3.50), Jas. Moss, Victoria.

Pears, Osbond's, summer—1st ($2.50), W. Arthur, Ladners ; 2nd ($1.50), Jubilee Farm, Ladners.

Plums, Peach—1st ($2.50), Jubilee Farm, Ladners ; 2nd ($1.50), J. Kirkland, Ladners ; 3rd ($1), W. Knight, Popcum.

Plums, Bradshaw—1st ($2.50), Jubilee Farm, Ladners.

Plums, Imp. Gage—1st ($2.50), Jubilee Farm, Ladners.

Peaches, Alexander—1st ($2.50), Hon. John Robson, Victoria.

Peaches, Early Crawford—1st ($2.50) J. Whitfield, Victoria ; 2nd ($1.50), C. E. Renouf, Victoria.

Currants, red—1st ($1.50), J. Whitfield, Victoria ; 2nd ($1), Jubilee Farm, Ladners.

Currants, white—1st ($1.50), Jubilee Farm, Ladners.

Currants, black—1st ($1.50), J. Whitfield, Victoria ; 2nd ($1), Jubilee Farm, Ladners.

Blackberries—1st ($1.50), Jas. Moss, Victoria.

Cherries, Duke—1st ($1.50), J. Lister, Westminster.

Quince—1st ($1.50), G. W. Henry, Port Hammond.

Raspberries—1st ($1.50), J. Whitfield, Victoria ; 2nd ($1), C. E. Renouf, Victoria.

Fruit, collection, bottled—1st ($5), J. Whitfield, Victoria.

Beans, wax— 1st ($2), C. E. Renouf, Victoria ; 2nd ($1.50), H. A. Hicks, Ladners; 3rd ($1), Jas. Moss, Victoria.

Beans, broad—1st ($2), C. E. Renouf, Victoria ; 2nd ($1.50), W. Arthur, Ladners ; 3rd ($1), Jubilee Farm, Ladners.

Beans, Scarlet Runner—1st ($2), T. McNeely, Ladners ; 2nd ($1.50), W. Arthur, Ladners.

Beets, long—1st ($2), W. Arthur, Ladners; 2nd ($1.50), Jubilee Farm, Ladners; 3rd ($1), H. A. Hicks, Ladners.

Beets, round—1st ($2), Jubilee Farm, Ladners; 2nd ($1.50), G. A. McTavish, Victoria; 3rd ($1), T. McNeely, Ladners.

Carrots, Horn—1st ($2), H. A. Hicks, Ladners; 2nd ($1,50), W. Arthur, Ladners; 3rd ($1), H. Henly, Clover Point.

Carrots, long—1st ($2), H. A. Hicks, Ladners; 2nd ($1.50), G. W. Henry, Port Hammond; 3rd ($1), W. Arthur, Ladners.

Celery, white—1st ($2), G. A. McTavish, Victoria.

Celery, red—1st ($2), Jas. Moss, Victoria.

Corn, sweet—1st ($2), H. Henly, Clover Point; 2nd ($1.50), T. McNeely, Ladners; 3rd ($1), G. W. Henry, Port Hammond.

Cucumbers, 2—1st ($2), E. Nash, Westminster; 2nd ($1.50), G. A. McTavish, Victoria; 3rd ($1), W. Dodds, Victoria.

Cucumbers, Gerkins—1st ($2), W. Arthur, Ladners.

Cabbage, summer—1st ($2), T. McNeely, Ladners; 2nd ($1.50), W. Arthur, Ladners; 3rd ($1), H. A. Hicks, Ladners.

Cauliflower—1st ($2), G. A. McTavish, Victoria; 2nd ($1.50), W. Dodds, Victoria; 3rd ($1), W. Arthur, Ladners.

Lettuce—1st ($2), T. McNeely, Ladners; 2nd ($1.50), H. Henly, Clover Point, 3rd ($1), C. E. Renouf, Victoria.

Melons, Musk—1st ($2), F. Nash, Westminster.

Onions, red—1st ($2.50), W. Dodds, Ladners; 2nd ($2), W. Arthur, Victoria.

Onions, white—1st ($2), T. McNeely, Ladners; 2nd ($1.50), H. N. Rich, Ladners; 3rd ($1), W. H. Mawdsley, Plumpers Pass.

Onions, yellow—1st ($2), H. Henly, Clover Point; 2nd ($1.50), W. Cox, Clover Point; 3rd ($1), H. A. Hicks, Ladners.

Parsnips—1st ($2), T. McNeely, Ladners; 2nd ($1.50), Jubilee Farm, Ladners; 3rd ($1), H. Henly, Clover Point.

Potatoes, peek—1st ($2), Jubilee Farm, Ladners; 2nd ($1.50), H. A. Hicks, Ladners; 3rd ($1), G. W. Henry, Port Hammond.

Potatoes, collection—1st ($3), Jas. Moss, Victoria.

Peas, in pod—1st ($2), G. A. McTavish, Victoria; 2nd ($1.50), C. E. Renouf, Victoria; 3rd ($1), J. Kirkland, Victoria.

Peas, quart—1st ($2), W. Dodds, Victoria; 2nd ($1.50), J. Kirkland, Victoria; 3rd ($1), J. Whitfield, Victoria.

Rhubarb—1st ($2), Jubilee Farm, Ladners; 2nd ($1.50), G. W. Henry, Port Hammond; 3rd ($1), Jas. Moss, Victoria.

Salsify—1st ($2), Jubilee Farm, Ladners.

Squash, summer—1st ($2), G. W. Henry, Port Hammond.

Squash, scalloped—1st ($2), Jubilee Farm, Ladners.

Turnips, table, 6—1st ($2), Jubilee Farm, Ladners; 2nd ($1.50), G. A. McTavish, Victoria; 3rd ($1), W. Arthur, Ladners.

Vegetable Marrow—1st ($2), H. N. Rich, Ladners; 2nd ($1.50), H. Henly, Clover Point; 3rd ($1), Jubilee Farm, Ladners.

Vegetables, collection—1st ($5), H. Henly, Clover Point; 2nd ($3), W. Dodds, Victoria; 3rd ($2), C. E. Renouf, Victoria.

SPECIALS.

Hollyhocks—1st ($2), Jas. Moss, Victoria.

Sweet Peas—1st ($2), Jas. Moss, Victoria.

Sunflower, double—1st ($2), Jas. Moss, Victoria.

4 pots Lobelia—1st ($2), J. R. Anderson, Victoria.

Basket Musk—1st ($2), J. R. Anderson, Victoria.

34 pots Ferns—1st ($2), J. R. Anderson, Victoria.

2 pots plants—1st ($2), J. R. Anderson, Victoria.

Fig plant—1st ($2), C. E. Renouf, Victoria.

Chicory—1st ($2), C. E. Renouf, Victoria.

Beans—1st ($2), H. Henly, Clover Point; 2nd ($1.50), H. A. Hicks, Ladners.

Hollyhocks, 2nd ($1.50), G. A. McTavish, Victoria.

———

VANCOUVER, November 3rd, 1891.—Quarterly meeting Directors of Horticultural Society and Fruit Growers' Association.—Present, W. J. Harris, Hammond (president), in chair; John Kirkland, Ladners (first vice-president); O. D. Sweet, Richmond (second vice-president); E. Hutcherson, Ladners; G. G. McKay, city; N. Butchart, Port Moody; T. Wilson, Harrison; W. J. Brandrith, North Arm; P. Latham, T. R. Pearson, New Westminster; A. W. Ross, M.P., Winnipeg; T. W. Clark, city.

Minutes of August 12th, 1891, were read and, on motion, confirmed. Correspondence was read and ordered to be filed.

Moved by Mr. Sweet, seconded by Mr. Hutcherson, Resolved that Mr. Bales and Mr. Broadwell be requested to furnish the association some scions and information re apples previously exhibited by them.

Discussion on packages took place, taken part in by E. Hutcherson, T. W. Clark, T. R. Pearson, P. Latham. An improvement in packing was considered most necessary.

Programme for annual meeting was adopted—

The annual meeting will be held in the Board of Trade rooms, Vancouver, on Wednesday and Thursday, 13th and 14th January, 1892, commencing at 3 o'clock p.m. on Wednesday.

President's Address. . . . . .W. J. Harris
Secretary-Treasurer's Report. . . . .
British Columbia Fruit in the East—Impressions of 1891—
      R. E. Cosnell, Vancouver, and A. C. Wells, Chilliwhack
Canning and Preserving Fruit. . . . . . .Okel & Morris, Victoria ; Fraser Valley
      Canning Co., Chilliwhack ; Walter Taylor, Vancouver
Plums and Prunes . . . . John Kirkland, Ladners
A Plea for our Native Flowering Shrubs . . . . .T. Wilson, Harrison River
Bee Culture. . . . . .R. L. Codd, Hatzie
Bartlett Pear. . . . . .E. Hutcherson, Ladners
Hop-Growing. . . . . .Wilson & Broe, Alder Grove
Gardens . . . . .Peter Latham, New Westminster
Bee Culture. . . . . .J. S. Smith, Chilliwhack
Exhibitions. . . . . .T. R. Pearson, New Westminster
British Columbia as a Fruit Growing Country in comparison with Ontario —
               G. W. Henry
Preparation of Orchards, E. Hutcherson, Ladners, and N. Butchart, Pt. Moody
Tree Planting. . . . . .W. J. Brandrith, North Arm
Fruit Packages . . . . .T. W. Clark, Vancouver

Members and others having choice samples of fruit, or any un-named or mis-named varieties, are requested to exhibit same for examination or naming at the meeting.

The best possible efforts will be màde to answer, or obtain answers to, questions on fruit growing asked by members and others.

The answers received to questions circulated throughout the province will be presented. Parties having received the question sheets will please fill in and return same.

On motion of Mr. Hutcherson, seconded by Mr. Sweet, Resolved that above programme be adopted : That thanks of association be presented to Board of Trade, and that a request be made for their rooms for the annual meeting.

Meeting adjourned.

————

VANCOUVER, January 13th, 1892.—Annual meeting of Horticultural Society and Fruit Growers' Association.—Present, W. J. Harris, president, in chair ; G. W. Henry, Hammond ; Thos. Cunningham, P. Latham, New Westminster ; W. J. Brandrith, North Arm ; J. H. Bent, Chilliwhack ; Tom Wilson, Harrison ; W. J. Henry, Vancouver ; John White, Hammond ; N. Butchart, Port Moody ; Wm. Morris, Victoria; J. T. Wilkinson, Chilliwhack ; Wm. Wintemute, Vancouver ; T. J. Trapp, A. C. Wilson, New Westminster ; F. S. Timberlake, Mission City ; J. H. Secord, G. G. McKay, Vancouver ; W. H. DeWolf, Chilliwhack.

The minutes, having been published, were taken as read and, on motion,. were confirmed.

Secretary-treasurer presented financial statement, which was referred to committee of Messrs. Thos. Cunningham and G. W. Henry.

Secretary read answers and suggestions.

Mr. Chadsey asked what kind of prunes were most valuable for drying. Mr. Cunningham said Italian or Fellenberg and German ; Petite Prune de Agen are unsuitable for this climate. Mr. Henry confirmed this.

Mr. H. Ferguson's suggestions re packing, etc., and matters of packages generally, were referred to committee of Messrs. W. J. Brandrith, A. C. Wilson, P. Latham, Thos. Cunningham, G. W. Henry and N. Butchart.

Moved by Mr. Cunningham, seconded by Mr. Henry, That this society adopt the Californian and Oregon sizes of apple and pear boxes, which are as follows :   Apple box, $20\frac{1}{2} \times 10 \times 12$ inside ; ends, $\frac{5}{8}$; tops, bottoms and sides, $\frac{1}{4}$—40 lbs.   Pear box, $18\frac{1}{2} \times 11\frac{3}{4} \times 8\frac{1}{2}$ inside ; ends, $\frac{3}{4}$; covers and sides, $\frac{1}{4}$—40 lbs. :   And that we furnish the various saw mills and box factories of this action, requesting all manufacturers of boxes to conform to this standard.

Moved by Mr. G. W. Henry, seconded by Mr. Cunningham, Resolved that the answers given to questions sent out be referred to committee to report to-morrow.   Committee—Messrs. W. J. Brandrith, A. C. Wilson, P. Latham, Thos. Cunningham, G. W. Henry and N. Butchart.

Mr. R. E. Gosnell read a paper on British Columbia Fruit in the East— Impressions of 1891.

Moved by G. W. Henry, seconded by Mr. Morris, Resolved that the thanks of the association be presented to Mr. Gosnell for his able paper.

Mr. Morris, of Okell & Morris, Victoria, read a paper on Canning and Preserving Fruit.   Mr. Latham asked if the Blenheim Orange Apples were much grown, and Mr. Butchart answered yes, at Port Moody.

Mr. Bent hoped to hear varieties of apples named by Mr. Morris as most suitable.   Mr. Morris said the Red Astrachan was a good apple.

Moved by Mr. Cunningham, seconded by Mr. Gosnell, Resolved that the thanks of the association be presented to Mr. Morris for his excellent-paper.

Mr. Cunningham said French prunes were the least profitable, and that it was madness to put an orchard under grass.

Mr. Morris said clear skin fruit, free from specks, are much preferable, He submitted samples of yellow egg plum, and said they (the firm) had orders for fifty thousand dozen of these last year, and can sell all they can put up. and will put up all they are able to secure.   Apples produced specked are depreciated 50% by the specks—more so if they were used for jellying. A specked apple is injured in quality and flavor.

Mr. Kirkland, being absent, sent a paper, which was read by the secretary; subject—Plums and Prunes.

Mr. Cunningham thought the splitting might be caused by grafting on to peach stalk. Mr. Latham suggested following as a remedy or check to bark bursting: Take north side of tree and run a knife through first bark in two places. He also stated that root pruning is done to bring young trees into bearing—one side is done each year.

Mr. Butchart asked what would cause the non-bearing of cherry trees he has had for some nine years; they bloom, partly form fruit and drop off.

Mr. Wilson read his paper on A Plea for our Native Flowering Plants.

Moved by Mr. G. W. Henry, seconded by Mr. Brandrith, Resolved that the thanks of the association be presented to Mr. Wilson for his paper.

Mr. R. L. Codd, Hatzic, who was unable to be present, sent a paper on Bee Culture, which was read by Mr. G. W. Henry.

Moved by Mr. Bent, seconded by Mr. Cunningham, Resolved that the thanks of the association be presented to Mr. Codd.

Mr. John L. Broe was not present, but a letter from him on Hop-Growing was read by the secretary.

Auditors reported the accounts of the association as correct, with $149.54 on hand.

Moved by Mr. Wilson, seconded by Mr. Latham, Resolved that report of auditors be adopted.

ELECTION OF OFFICERS.

Moved by Mr. Brandrith, seconded by Mr. G. W. Henry, Resolved, unanimously, that W. J. Harris, Port Hammond, be president.

Moved by A. H. B. Macgowan, seconded by G. W. Henry, Resolved unanimously, that Thos. Cunningham be first vice-president.

Moved by Mr. Henry, seconded by Mr. Wilson, Resolved, unanimously, that N. Butchart be second vice-president.

Moved by Mr. Henry, seconded by Mr. Cunningham, Resolved, unanimously, that A. H. B. Macgowan be secretary-treasurer.

DIRECTORS FOR 1892.

Agassiz, GEORGE A. BEEBE
" T. A. SHARP
Ashcroft, EX-GOVERNOR CORNWALL
Burton Prairie, H. P. BALES
Cache Creek, C. A. SEMLIN, M.P.P.
Chilliwhack, I. KIPP
" A. C. WELLS
" J. H. BENT
Comox, J. A. HALIDAY
Cowichan, J. BRADWELL
Donald, A. W. MANUEL
Esquimalt, HON. C. E. POOLEY
Hatzic, R. L. CODD
Hammond, G. W. HENRY
Harrison River, T. WILSON
Howe Sound, GEO. GIBSON
Kamloops, H. McCUTCHEON
" J. A. MARA
Ladner's Landing, E. HUTCHERSON
" " J. KIRKLAND
" " W. H. LADNER
Langley, JOHN MAXWELL
Port Haney, HECTOR FERGUSON
Port Moody, NORVAL BUTCHART
Richmond, O. D. SWEET
Saanich, J. D. BRYANT
Salt Spring Island,
J. P. BOOTH, M.P.P.
Spallumcheen, DONALD GRAHAM
Spence's Bridge, JOHN MURRAY
Squamish, E. B. MADILL
Sumas, ALLEN EVANS
Surrey, J. PUNCH, M.P.P.
Vancouver, J. M. BROWNING

Langley, JAS. McADAM
Lillooet, C. A. PHAIR
Lulu Island, J. RUPERT FOSTER
Maple Ridge, W. J. HARRIS
" JOHN WHITE
Matsqui, C. B. SWORD
" H. F. PAGE
Mission City, F. S. TIMBERLAKE.
Mayne Island, T. R. FIGG
Nicola, JOHN CLAPERTON
North Arm, W. J. BRANDRITH
New Westminster,
" PETER LATHAM
" THOS. CUNNINGHAM
" A. C. WILSON
" T. R. PEARSON
" MARSHALL SINCLAIR
Okanagan, ALFRED POSTILL
" GEO. WHELAN
" LORD ABERDEEN
" HON. MAJORIBANKS
Pender Island, W. GRIMMER
Vancouver, G. G. McKAY
" R. E. GOSNELL
" R. T. ROBINSON
" WALTER TAYLOR
" A. H. B. MACGOWAN
Victoria, G. A. McTAVISH
" D. W. HIGGINS
MR. JAY
D. KER
" C. E. RENOUF
" W. H. BAINBRIDGE

Moved by Mr. Thos. Cunningham, seconded by Mr. G. W. Henry, Resolved that Hons. Hugh Nelson, John Robson, F. G. Vernon, J. H. Turner, Theo. Davie, and David Oppenheimer, Esq., be, and they are, hereby elected honorary members of this association.

Moved by Mr. Bent, seconded by Mr. Cunningham, Resolved that next quarterly meeting of the directors be held at Chilliwhack.

Moved by Mr. Latham, seconded by Mr. T. Wilson, That next exhibition be held at Vancouver on or about 10th August—time to be finally fixed at May meeting.

Amendment moved by Mr. Latham, seconded by Mr. Wintemute, That exhibition be held first week in July.

Amendment put and lost ; original motion put and declared carried.

Moved by Mr. Macgowan, seconded by Mr. Brandrith, Resolved that G. W. Henry, E. Hutcherson, R. T. Robinson, Thos. Cunningham and P. Latham be a committee on exhibition ; and, That the Mayor, F. Cope, of Vancouver, Messrs. J. M. Browning, D. Oppenheimer, R. T. Robinson, R. E. Gosnell, G. G. McKay, Walter Taylor and A. H. B. Macgowan be a special exhibition committee.

Moved by Mr. White, seconded by Mr. Brandrith, Resolved that a supplement on pests, insects and remedies be added to annual report.

Moved by Mr. Cunningham, seconded by Mr. Henry, Resolved that a committee of Thos. Cunningham, G. W. Henry, E. Hutcherson and W. J. Brandrith be appointed with the secretary to compile the annual report and supplement to same.

Letter, of January 12th, 1892, from H. P. Bales *re* naming of his apple which had been before the association.

Moved by Mr. Cunningham, seconded by Mr. G. W. Henry, Resolved that the name of H. P. Bales' apple as previously discussed as the "British Columbia Apple" be confirmed.

Moved by Mr. Macgowan, seconded by Mr. Cunningham, Resolved that a vote of thanks be presented to Capt. J C. Rounding, Sydney, N.S.W., for the interest he has manifested in our association and for the valuable information received from him.

Mr. G. W. Henry read his paper on British Columbia as a Fruit Growing Country in comparison with Ontario.

Moved by Mr. Cunningham, seconded by Mr. Bent, Resolved that the thanks of this association be presented to Mr. Henry for his valuable paper.

Moved by Mr. T. Cunningham, seconded by Mr. T. Wilson, Resolved that the annual meeting of the Horticultural Society and Fruit Growers' Association of British Columbia desires to place on record its appreciation of the valuable financial aid received from the government of the province, and would respectfully request that an appropriation of $1000 be placed in estimates for 1892-93.

Mr. Butchart read his paper on Preparation of Orchards.

Moved by Mr. Henry, seconded by Mr. Wilson, Resolved that the thanks of the association be presented to Mr. Butchart for his paper.

Mr. W. J. Brandrith read his paper on Tree Planting, showing samples of good and inferior work.   Mr. Cunningham considered trunk should be shorter than that shown, viz., four feet. Californians are now making eighteen inches the standard from ground to branches. Mr. Brandrith said he took care to have all roots resting well on ground. Tree shown was three years old last spring and was then cut back. Mr. Brandrith gave an exhibition of pruning. His work was discussed by G. W. Henry, P. Latham, T. Cunningham and T. Wilson.

Moved by Mr. Henry, seconded by Mr. Latham, Resolved that a vote of thanks be presented to Mr. Brandrith for his paper and exhibition.

Re packages for small plants, moved by Mr. Macgowan, seconded by Mr. W. J. Brandrith, Resolved that Messrs. Cunningham, Henry and Hutcherson be a committee to select packages after the society has received samples and price lists; meantime, parties requiring packages are requested to send quantity and kind to the secretary.

Moved by Mr. Brandrith, seconded by Mr. Cunningham, Resolved that committee appointed to consider questions and answers be authorized to have their decisions incorporated in annual report, and also to answer questions asked by the different parties.

Mr. T. Wilson read a paper on Plant Lice.

Mr. Butchart asked what the members would think of planting dwarf apple trees.

Mr. Brandrith said he had sold ex-alderman Costello forty standard apple trees and twelve dwarf. Thirty-three of the standards are doing well, but the dwarf trees have never budded.

Mr. Henry had good success with dwarf apples planted in British Columbia.

Mr. Harris said dwarf apple trees had done best of any with him. The fruit, he said, was good. Dwarf, 20-oz. Pippin, Maiden Blush, Haas and others had also done well.

Moved by Mr. Cunningham, seconded by Mr. Wilson, Resolved that the secretary be authorized to call for tenders for printing annual report.

HORTICULTURAL SOCIETY AND FRUIT GROWERS' ASSOCIATION OF BRITISH COLUMBIA IN ACCOUNT WITH

A. H. B. MACGOWAN, - - SECRETARY-TREASURER.

Nov. 30. By Balance on hand	$ 48.69
„ Government Grant	1000.00
„ Donation, C. E. Renouf	13.00
„ Fees from 87 members	170.00
	$1231.69

To Prizes Paid.. $ 369.00
  ,, Printing and ads.. 270.25
  ,, *Canadian Horticulturist*, 88 members 70.40
  ,, Postage, Cards, etc 19.50
  ,, Secretary, 12 months................................. 360.00
        Balance.. 149.69

                                              $1231.69

(Signed)   W. J. HARRIS, President.
                  JOHN KIRKLAND, Vice-President.
                  A. H. B. MACGOWAN, Secretary.

Audited and found correct,
        (Signed)   THOMAS CUNNINGHAM, ⎫
                                               ⎬ Auditors.
                        G. W. HENRY,   ⎭

In Memoriam

MR. JOHN LISTER,

Who was born at Oweston, Yorkshire, England, in 1821, where he was engaged in agriculture and horticulture until 1864, when he removed to Halifax, where he followed the nursery business and landscape gardening until 1884, when he left there for British Columbia. After spending three years on a farm in Surrey municipality, he removed to New Westminster, where he resumed his old profession, in which he continued until his death on October 12th, 1891.

In the death of Mr. Lister the association loses an honored and active director, and one whose place will be hard to fill, and his co-workers desire to place on record their appreciation of his labors in this connection.

Answers to Question Lists.

In November, 1891, a list of 40 questions and about as many sub-questions were circulated throughout the province, and the results are given below as answers received from districts named.

AGASSIZ.

District from Sea, Bird to Farr's Bluff: About 16 acres under orchards planted previous to 1890. During 1890, 7 acres; 1891, 5 acres. Between 5,000 and 6,000 acres taken up; about same quantity in Indian reserves. Soil, river sediment on loose ground, giving splendid drainage. Climate, moist and cool in summer, moist and mild in winter. Degrees of heat, 65 to 85; cold, 20 to 40, Farhen. Snow falls occasionally. Nights cool.

The most successful fruits are plums, pears, cherries, apricots, strawberries, currants, raspberries and some kinds of apples, viz., Red Astrachan for summer, Gravenstein for autumn and Baldwin for winter are most satisfactory. Hazel nuts are found wild, also limited quantities of cranberries. Sugar beets do well, tomatoes moderately well. Hops set out this year are doing remarkably well. Wild strawberries, salmon berries, raspberries, blackberries and crab apples grow.

In wild flowers we have tiger and several other lilies, lupin orchids, moccasin flower, syringa and rugged robin.

Following pests have appeared: Caterpillars, forest tent caterpillars, oyster shell bark louse, mildew on gooseberries and green aphis, apple tree caterpillar, apple and pear blight on leaf. A large gray and white bug, about ½ inch long, eats the leaf and injures tree very much.

Want remedy for blight on apple tree bark.

Cultivating orchard in buckwheat has given me good results, keeping the ground mellow.

Low headed trees do best.

Packages of sawed lumber from Popcum mills at cost of about 13 cents for 50 pound box are used.

Best results are from home grown, yearling stock.

Market, local. Market can be improved by cheaper transportation and fewer middle men.

Recommend having arbor day.

ASCHCROFT.

Soil, rich loam and heavy whitish clay.

High lands give best results.

Climate, Degrees of heat, 100 in shade ; degrees of cold, 25 below zero. Light snow fall, say 18 inches.

Most successful varieties of fruit : Apples and plums, all small fruits, especially currants. Duchess of Oldenburg we find best autumn apple and Northern Spy best winter. Wild cranberries are found in considerable quantities. Tomatoes ripen.

Hops are produced with great success.

Following wild fruits are found : Service berry, salmon berry, cranberry, huckleberry, gooseberry, currants, strawberries, cherries, and others ; also a great variety of wild flowers. Grapes seem to do well and ripen thoroughly.

The chief pests are, green aphis, grasshoppers, cut worms and the spotted blister beetle, which should be brushed off tree into coal oil tins. Cut worms are searched for early in morning, and trees are syringed for aphis.

Orchard surface should be kept stirred up and free from weeds, with occasional irrigation through drills by the rows of trees.

Low headed grown trees do best.

Eastern stock has done well.

Annual exhibition is too early in season.

CHILLIWACK.

Acreage under orchards : Previous to 1890, 9 ; planted in 1890, 19 ; planted in 1891, 33.

Soil : Sandy loam, gravel bottom, alluvial deposit washed from mountains.

Degrees of heat, 90 ; cold, 22. Snow falls occasionally. Nights cool. Winds light.

Most successful fruits are, apples, pears, plums, peaches, cherries, strawberries, raspberries, gooseberries, currants, blackberries, prunes, quince.

The following are most successful fruits : Apples—summer, Early June, Astrachan, Duchess of Oldenburg ; autumn, Bellefleur, Munson, Gravenstein, King ; winter, Baldwin, Greening, Russet.

Pears : Most of well known varieties do well. Crab apples : Hyslop and Transcendent. Peach : Hales, Crawfords, Alexanders, Plums : Bradshaw, Lombard, Egg, Gage. Wild cranberries abound. Sugar beets do well. Tomatoes ripen. Melons are produced when properly cared for.

In wild fruits are found, raspberries, blackberries, strawberries, gooseberries, salmon berries, blueberries, bramble berries, whortle and currants. .

In wild flowers we have various kinds of lilies and other bulbous flowers, and a large variety of flowering shrubs.

We are not much troubled with pests.

Best results are from cultivated orchards. We head our trees high.

In packing, a box has been used, costing 12 to 16 cents each. Think a half barrel would be preferable.

Careful picking and sizing of fruit ought to be observed.

Local and eastern stock do well.

Needs of district : Buyers who know how to pack, and insist on good packing : reduction of express and freight rates, and employment of a good lecturer.

Recommend having arbor day.

LADNERS LANDING.

Delta Municipality, 40,000 acres.

Orchards planted previous to 1890, 50 acres ; planted during 1890, 60 acres ; planted during 1891, 40 acres.

All land is taken up.

Soil : Deep black loam, clay sub-soil. River bottoms produce best fruits.

Most successful fruits are, apples, plums, pears, prunes, strawberries, currants, gooseberries. In kinds the following do best :

Apples—Summer, Yellow Transparent, Red Astrachan, Keswic Codlin ; autumn, Gravenstein, Duchess, Wealthy, Blenheim Orange ; winter, Baldwin, Canada Red, McIntosh Red, Golden Russet.

Pears—Summer, Madeline, Clapp's Favorite ; autumn, Bartlett, Duchess d'Angouleine, Louise, Bonne de Jersey ; winter, Beurre Clairgeau, Beurre d'Anjou, Vicar of Wakefield.

Crab apples—Transcendent, Hyslop.

Peaches—Early Crawford, Alexander.

Plums—Bradshaw, Red Egg.

Prunes— Italian.

Cherries—Royal Ann.

Apricots—St. Catherines.

Strawberries—Improved Jucunda.

Raspberries—Cuthberts.

Gooseberries—Oregon Champion.

Currants—Hay's Red.

Blackberries—Kittatiny.

Quince—Orange.

Figs—growing but not fruited.

Medlar—growing but not fruited.

Almonds —4 varieties produced.

Filberts—doing well.

Walnuts—doing well.

Chestnuts—7 varieties, not yet fruited.

Hazel—successful.

Wild cranberries—grow on about 6,000 acres.

Sugar beets—succeed.

Tomatoes—ripen.

Hops—very successfully raised.

In wild fruits we have salmon berries, crab apples, black raspberries.

We are troubled with the following pests : Forest tent caterpillar, pear or cherry, tree slug, oyster shell bark louse, mildew (light), green aphis, vegetable mould (light), moss.

Remedies—Concentrated lye for oyster shell louse and moss ; Paris green for tent caterpillars ; coal oil emulsion for green aphis.

Cultivated orchards do best. Our best method is cultivate to roots. Heading back system of pruning most advisable. Low headed trees do best.

Slab covering under-drainage has given good results.

In packages we use 24 box crates for strawberries ; 10 lb. boxes for currants ; 12 quart baskets for pears, procured in the east.

Would recommend that a committee be appointed to arrange for standard package.

Inspection is recommended.

An arbor day advisable.

Local grown trees most satisfactory.

Market unsatisfactory. Could be improved by bringing grower and consumer closer together.

Question—Are North-west markets satisfactory, and for what fruits?

PORT HAMMOND.

Municipality of Maple Ridge.

Orchards planted previous to 1890, 200 acres; planted during 1890, 30 acres; planted during 1891, 40 acres.

Soil is of all descriptions, from richest river bottom to lightest high land. Land best adapted to fruit strong, sandy loam. High land gives finest flavor and best colored fruit.

Climate: Mild, abundance of rain. Degrees of heat, greatest, 90 in shade; degrees of cold, zero about coldest. Snow falls some winters, 2 feet. Nights cool. Winds seldom strong.

All kinds of hardy fruits prosper. Most successful are apples. Summer, Gravenstein and Duchess of Oldenburg; autumn, Wealthy and King of Tompkins; winter, Northern Spy, Golden Russet, Ben Davies, Baldwin, Stark.

Pears—Summer, Bartlett, Clapp's Favorite; autumn, Clairgeau, Howell Sheldon; winter, Beurre d'Anjou, Easter, Lawrence.

Crab apples—Transcendent and Hyslop.

Peaches — Alexander, Early Rivers, Crawford, Wager, Schumaker, Waterloo.

Grapes—Moyer, Worden, Delaware, Moore's Diamond, Moore's Early Niagara.

Strawberries—All kinds do well. Sharpless and Crescent principally grown.

Raspberries—Red varieties, especially Cuthbert and Marlboro'.

Gooseberries—Industry, Smith's Improved, Oregon Champion, Downing.

Currants—Fay's Prolific, cherry, white grape, Lee's Prolific.

Blackberries—Taylor, Snyder, Kittatiny, Lawlor.

Quince—Orange, Rhea's Mammoth.

Fig trees we find winter kills badly.

Almond trees do well but not yet fruited.

Filberts are excellent.

Walnuts are excellent.

Chestnuts—doing well, but not yet fruited.

Hazels—do well.

Cranberries—grow in abundance.

Sugar beets—do well.

Tomatoes ripen.

Melons are not very successfully grown.

Hops are very successfully produced.

In wild fruits we have raspberries, strawberries, gooseberries, currants, cherries, crab apples, and wild flowers too numerous to name.

In pests we have met pear or cherry tree slug, wooly maple bark louse, mildew, green aphis, borers, vegetable mould, moss, and injury is done apple trees by continued freezing and thawing in winter, and hard frost after warm weather.

Remedies—For aphis, kerosene emulsion also air slacked lime; for pear or cherry tree slug, above remedies or liquid Helebore. Pyrethrum dusted on is also effectual. For moss or borers and other insects on bark, a wash of soft soap is best remedy.

Best results are from continued cultivation during growing season. Trees in grass fail almost entirely while young. Old trees do fairly in grass if land is not too dry. In pruning would advise cutting back all overgrown shoots, or, what is better, nipping back of young shoots during summer when growing too long, and a well opened head. In high or low headed trees we find neither extreme advisable; too high heads give too much exposure to wind and attack of insects; too low prevent sufficient sun and air from getting under and through the tree, which causes much of the fruit to be inferior unless trees are far apart. $3\frac{1}{2}$ to 4 feet from ground is best height to begin to branch from.

In packages we use baskets from Ontario for small fruits, and 50 pound boxes from mills of this province for apples.

It is a matter of greatest importance that a standard package be adopted, particularly for winter apples. For summer apples and soft fruits generally, baskets or small boxes could be used. Selling by weight ought to be carried out.

Suggestions: Better selecting of varieties when planting, taking better care of orchards, closer culling of fruit, putting no imperfect specimens in the packages, better packages, more care in selection of fruit and packing.

· Arbor day would be well received.

Local or home grown stock gives excellent success. Eastern stock very satisfactory when from reliable parties direct. Oregon and Washington stock not in favor.

Market would be improved by more and better cared-for orchards, and greater care in the putting up of fruit.

PORT HANEY.

Township 12, New Westminster District.

Soil: River land, clay, quicksand and mica. High land, stiff clay sub-soil with deposit about 2 feet of sub-soil. Find the high land gives best quality, and low land produces greatest quantity.

Most of fruits do well, apples, pears, plums, prunes, cherries, etc.

Following kinds are most successful:

Apples—Summer, Red Astrachan, Early Harvest; autumn, Gravenstein, Duchess, Wealthy, King; winter, Northern Spy, Baldwin, Golden Russet, Yellow Bellefleur, Ben Davis.

Pears—Spring, Bartlett, Clapp's Favorite; autumn, Beurre d'Anjou, Howell, Bonne de Jersey, Keiffer; winter, Lawrence, W. Nelles.

Crab apples—**H**yslop.

Peaches—Early Crawford.

Prunes—Pond's Seedling.

Cranberries, wild—grow in large quantities.

Sugar beets—succeed well.

Tomatoes—ripen under favorable circumstances.

Hops are a decided success.

In wild fruits we have crab apples, strawberries, blackberries, salmon berries, huckleberries, etc.

Wild flowers abound.

Following pests have appeared: Caterpillars, codlin moth, oyster shell louse, mildew, green aphis, borers, apple tree caterpillar, moss, blights

Coal oil emulsion cures green aphis, and lye wash cures moss.

Orchards are mostly cultivated. We find root crops suit orchards, **and** peas seem to be beneficial where ground is too rough for roots.

Cedar underdrains have given good results.

50 pound boxes are used for apples,. They are better to be solid, perfectly covering the fruit, and be made of $\frac{3}{4}$ inch thick. Winter fruit for keeping should be packed in barrels. Would recommend inspection.

Local or home grown trees are best and cheapest.

The need of the district is information on fruit growing.

A lecturer should be sent round to deliver lectures on fruit growing, and give instructions in growing, picking and packing fruit.

I would suggest that Parliament be requested to pass a stringent law for the checking of the spreading and extermination of pests.

Would not advise having arbor day.

PORT MOODY.

Acreage under orchards, 24 acres ; planted during 1891, 9 acres.

Soil : Sandy loam. High lands give best results in fruit.

Degrees of heat, average, 70 ; degrees of cold, average, 1 to 10 below freezing. Snow fall, 1 to 8 inches. Have but little wind. Nights are cool.

We find the following to be the best :

Apples—Wealthy, Gravenstein, Duchess of Oldenburg, Ben Davis, Rhode Island, Greening, Mammoth, Baldwin.

Pears—Bartlett, Clapp's Favorite, Flemish Beauty, Beurre d'Anjou.

Crab apples—Montreal Beauty.

Peaches—Early Crawford.

Plums—Bradshaw.

Prunes—Italian and German.

Grapes—Concord.

Strawberries—Sharpless.

Raspberries—Large red.

Gooseberries—Industry.

Currants—Fay's Prolific.

Blackberries—Kittatiny.

Tomatoes ripen.

Hops do extra well.

In wild fruits we have salmon berries, huckleberries, blackberries and black raspberries.

Pests are caterpillars, hop plant louse.

Remedy—A wash of one can concentrated lye to five gallons of water applied with a long handled brush, but never when tree is growing.

Cultivated orchards are best. We use common cultivator in preference to plough which cuts roots of trees. We prune ⅓ to ½ previous year's growth, and keep open in centre.

Low headed trees are preferable.

Packages used are, for apples, boxes, 11x12x20. Would advise a standard package, 1lb. for small fruits, and I believe barrels would carry apples better than boxes.

Home grown stock is best.

Market is good.

Think position of things could be greatly improved by lower rates of interest, to enable clearing and preparation of land, which is expensive work in this country.

SALT SPRING ISLAND.

Land under orchards : Previous to 1890, 78 acres ; planted in 1890, 45 acres ; in 1891, 7 acres.

Soil : Sandy loam on hard clay sub-soil with bottom of black soil. We find that sandy loam with open sub-soil is best adapted for fruit, and high land the most preferable.

We have some winds.

We grow apples, pears, plums, cherries and peaches. The most successful kinds are :

Apples—Summer, Red Astrachan ; autumn, Gravenstein, King of Tompkins ; winter, Baldwin, Swarr, Lemon, Pippins, Bellefleurs.

Pears—Summer, Early Butter ; autumn, Bartlett, Flemish Beauty ; winter, Vicar of Wakefield.

Plums—Columbia.

Grapes—Concord.

Tomatoes ripen.

Hops grow well.

The following pests are met ; Forest tent caterpillar, green aphis, oyster shell bark louse, mildew, vegetable mould, moss, blights.

Remedies—Lye wash, soap-sud wash, but most successful is dog-fish oil.

Orchards, to be successful, must be cultivated.

In pruning, we cut well back.

Standard boxes should be used for apples and pears.

Home grown stock gives best results ; foreign stock often not true to name.

SHORTREED (ALDER GROVE).

Our soil is clay, with some gravel and sand sub-soil.   Best results in fruit are from high land.

Apples, pears, prunes, plums, berries, currants and most fruits do well, with best results from following kinds :

Apples—Summer, Red Astrachan ;   autumn, Gravenstein ;   winter, Greening, Blue Pearmain.

Pears—Summer, Bartlett and Clapp's Favorite ; autumn, Fall, Butter, Beurre d'Anjou ; winter, Winter, Nelles.

Crab Apples—Transcendent.

Peaches—Early Crawford.

Plums—Yellow Eggs, Columbia.

Prunes—Italian and Silver.

Cherries—Royal Ann, Black, Tartarian.

Apricots—Royal.

Nectarines—Boston.

Grapes—Concord.

Raspberries—Mammoth Cluster (black).

Gooseberries—English (large).

English Walnuts and Spanish Chestnuts prosper.

Wild cranberries grow in small quantities.

Hops are most successful.

In wild fruits we have dewberries, black raspberries, salmonberries, strawberries, huckleberries (red and black), high bush cranberries.

Pests are : Mildew, hop plant louse, apple borers. We did some spraying on hops which was successful.

Orchards should be cultivated ; the whole surface should be kept clear of weeds.

Fall pruning is best.

Medium high-headed trees are preferable, the better admitting of cultivation.

Cedar underdrainage has been successfully used.

Home grown stock most satisfactory.

We are making wine from raspberries and black currants, and if a market for same could be opened, this business could be made very valuable to the province. Superior wines can be produced here in great quantities at reasonable prices. Would like Fruit Growers' Association to open up a market for our wines.

STEVESTON.

Soil : Rich clay loam.

All the surrounding country gives good results in most kinds of fruit.

Find low lands best for small fruits.

Wild cranberries grow to a considerable extent.

Sugar beets do extra well.

Tomatoes ripen.

Writer knows of no pests.

We prune from the inside.

Cedar covering for underdrainage has given good satisfaction.

Local home grown nursery stock has been most successful.

Market is good.

Want of district : more fruit growers.

SUMAS.

About 25 acres under orchards. Land taken up : about 8000 acres.

Soil ; black loam and clay loam. If well drained, river bottom land gives best results.

Degrees of heat : greatest, 95. Degrees of cold : greatest, 5 below zero. Depth of snow : 8 inches some seasons. Winds prevail. Nights are cool.

Apples, pears, peaches, plums, prunes, quinces, gooseberries, currants, -etc., do well.

The most successful kinds are :

Apples—Summer, Red Astrachan, Grey Astrachan; autumn, Gravenstein, Porter's, Maiden's Blush, King of Tompkins; winter, Northern Spy, Golden Russet, Baldwin, Seek-no-Further, Roxbury Russet, Greening, Ben Davis, Lemon.

Pears—Bartlett.

Wild Hazel abounds.

Wild cranberries are found abundantly.

Sugar beets do splendidly.

Tomatoes ripen.

Melons are produced.

Hops grow well.

Wild brambleberries, black raspberries, strawberries, etc., are found.

The following pests exist : Caterpillar, apple tree caterpillar, moss.

In cultivation, would recommend liberal cultivation of soil for first ten years; after that, seed down with orchard grass, keeping top dressed with barnyard and chip manure.

My pruning I prefer doing in autumn after fruit is gathered, keeping tree well balanced to admit of light.

For heading I take a tree high enough to admit of a horse passing under.

Packages used are : For apples, boxes, heads 10x12, sides 22 inches ; got from saw mills, cost 18 cents, including nails and making. I would recommend the 150 pound barrel, same to be branded with packer's name

Would recommend an inspection

Would recommend having an arbor day.

Home grown trees give greatest satisfaction

Needs of district are education in kinds of fruit to plant for profit.

Qualities should be graded.

Prunes promising to be a large part of future crops, people ought to be posted on best kinds to plant.

VICTORIA CITY.

About 100 acres under orchards. All land near is taken up.

Soil : Sandy and clay loam.

Degrees of heat, max., 75 ; degrees of cold, min., 20.   Seldom any snow. Nights are cool.   Winds prevail.

Plums, cherries, apples, pears and all small fruits do well, following being most successful :

Apples—-Summer, Gravenstein, Red June ; autumn, King ; winter, Belle fleur, Spitzenberg.

Pears—Summer, Bartlett ; autumn, Seckle ; winter, Winter Nelles.

Crab apples—Siberian.

Peaches—Alexander, Crawford.

Prunes—German.

Apricots—Moorepark.

Grapes— Concord.

Strawberries—Sharpless,

Raspberries—Cuthbert.

Gooseberries--American varieties.

Blackberries--Snyder, Kittatiny.

Filberts, walnuts, chestnuts, hickory nuts and hazel nuts grow satisfactorily.

Tomatoes ripen.

Pests met are ; Caterpillars, codlin moth, oyster shell bark louse, mildew, green aphis, borers, moss. Woolly aphis unusually bad this year on apples. Cut worms abundant. A grub or worm very destructive to Narcissi bulbs have only been seen in larvæl form yet.

Remedy—Best insecticide fir tree oil.

For city fruit trees low heads are preferable.

Underdrainage has given satisfactory results where tried.

A standard package should be adopted, and packers should be more careful in selecting packages, also in culling fruit.

Local grown trees succeed best.   Prefer Oregon to eastern or European stock.

Market is local and fairly satisfactory.

YALE.

About 150 acres from 8 miles below Hope to Yale under orchards.

Soil : Sand and gravel loam ; no clay.

Degrees of heat, 108 in shade ; degrees of cold, 10 below zero about low-est. Snow falls 3 to 6 feet. Nights cool.

Summer, autumn and winter apples and pears do well, particularly the later varieties. Crab apples, early peaches, plums, cherries, apricots, early grapes, strawberries, raspberries, currants and blackberries prosper.

Walnuts, chestnuts, hickory nuts, hazel nuts and butter nuts grow.

Sugar beets do well.

Tomatoes ripen.

Hops do splendidly.

Wild fruits and flowers abound.

Pests found are, caterpillars, codlin moth, black knot, mildew, apple tree caterpillar and moss, also a green spider on plants.

Remedies—Mixed powder, ashes, tobacco smoke.

Cultivated orchards do best.

Local grown trees give best satisfaction, Oregon next.

Market is local ; not very satisfactory.

Papers Read before the Association.

LABELLING.—NUMBERING *versus* NAMING.

PAPER PRESENTED AT DIRECTORS' MEETING, MAY 5TH, 1891.

Chairman and Gentlemen:

It is of the utmost importance that every tree in the orchard should be known, and a record kept of its doings ; in fact a full history of the tree ought to be in the possession of the orchardist. It is to lay before this meeting the plan of a system which, to some extent, meets the requirements of the case, that these few remarks are tendered.

Where the orchard is small, a map giving the position of each tree *might* be made, but this would only be suitable on small places, *or* where the orchard is large, the map would have to be made in sections ; but even this would entail more labor than the ordinary fruit grower has time for. Last fall I planted out over 1,000 trees, 500 apple among the rest. Before planting, the land was measured off into distances, and the pits dug, and each pit got a number ; after planting, the name of the tree planted in each hole was entered in a book against its corresponding number. The following table may help to make my meaning clearer :

No.	Name	Date of Planting.	Remarks.
1	Golden R.	Fall of 1890	Flowered in spring, 1891.
2	Baldwin	:: ::	·· ʺ ··

I claim this advantage for the numbering system, that it is simpler and saves labor, and in the event of a tree dying or being destroyed in any way, it can be replaced by any other, and no trouble with tallies writing, the name of the substitute can be entered in against its number.

In the remarks column anything can be written which is worth noting about any particular tree, and a complete history of the different trees kept.

My tallies are made of cedar, but I intend to have them made of zinc and the numbers put on with acid, so as to be almost indestructible with the weather.

Lisgar Farm,   TOM WILSON.
    Harrison River.

IMPRESSIONS OF B.C. FRUIT IN THE EAST.

R. E. GOSNELL.

To the President and Members of the B.C. Fruit Growers' Association:

GENTLEMEN,—My report on the British Columbia fruit at the eastern fairs must not be regarded as in any sense official, but purely an informal affair, and as conveying a few suggestions that may, or may not, be useful. It will be brief. I have not time to make an elaborate and detailed reference to the whole subject, with comparisons where eastern fruit is concerned, and my remarks of last year render it unnecessary.

To start with, the season in British Columbia was unfavorable to the best results for exhibition purposes. It was backward, say two weeks later than in former years, and to a large extent the crop was a failure compared with some previous crops. Notwithstanding these drawbacks, however, the collection of fruits was a good one, particularly that in bottles. Perhaps there was not as great variety of fruits as the year before. Some of the best specimens spoiled on the way, and several boxes that were shipped direct without being opened here, owing to imperfect packing, were useless when they reached Toronto.

Some disparaging remarks in the columns of the local press appeared, which I felt it my duty to refer to as follows in the report to the president of the Exhibition Association, who took pains himself to ascertain the truth of the assertions about the exhibition being a disgrace to the province, and from independent resources received quite a reverse verdict

At Toronto we were awarded a large space in a fairly favorable location, in the eastern half of the Natural History building, which was quite near to the main entrance and exits. Besides, placards were posted in every part of the grounds, directing the public to it, and a large streamer was placed over the main entrance pointing to it. The building itself is airy, roomy and well lighted. We occupied about 250 feet of wall space, 10 feet high, and about 1,000 square feet of table space, as well as considerable space surrounding the front entrance to the building, where the larger exhibits—timber, manufactured woods, coal, slate—were placed. The photographs, six in number, which were sent you, will give a better idea of the arrangement than I can convey here. Briefly, separate spaces were allotted to Victoria and district, Nanaimo, the Experimental Farm, Harrison valley, Westminster, Chilliwack, Delta, Westham Island, Lulu and Sea Islands, and Vancouver, arranged in the above order, with Victoria and Vancouver facing. With a liberal use of red and blue and white cottons, large views of the province, numerous large maple leaves, festoonings of cedar, flags and mottoes, together with the general arrangement of fruit, grains on the walls, and other exhibits, we succeeded, I think, in having a very attractive exhibit. I judge not only from my own appreciation of such matters, which might be considered as naturally biassed in favor of what was done under my own supervision, but from the comments of visitors, and from the thousands who poured in and who seemed to take a very eager interest in what they saw, and plied attendants with myriads of questions. Of course, residents of British Columbia who visited the fair were naturally more critical and less appreciative than strangers, because nothing appeared unusual to them, but unless they were not honest in the expression of their opinion, which would be a very unfair assumption indeed, they were all well pleased with what they saw. It must be remembered, too, that a baggage car, heavily laden, arrived on Monday evening, and the exhibits were required to be in place on Wednesday, which, in consideration of the amount of labor in handling, arranging and decorating, etc., several thousand individual articles, is deserving of some leniency, even if the eye of the fastidious were offended in a few of the details. However, notwithstanding the disparaging remarks which appeared in the local press, cowardly because anonymous, there are no apologies to offer, nor are any necessary. The press of Toronto and other cities whose representatives were frequent visitors, spoke in the highest terms and published much of interest concerning the province. Manitoba and the Northwest had a splendid exhibit, handled by the C. P. R., and one of which the west and all Canada should feel proud, but, while I do not admit that ours suffered depreciation by comparison, the former cost ten dollars where the British Columbia exhibit cost one, and had as many more men to look after and arrange it. Given the same appropriation, a similar number of men and equal facilities in other respects, British Columbia could far surpass the efforts of any other province in the Dominion in making a varied and effective display. The glassware alone for exhibiting the grains of the Northwest cost more than our exhibit altogether from first to last. And in regard to fruit, as Mr. Hill points out in his letter to you, it cannot be expected that fruit carried 3,000 miles will look as well three weeks after being pulled as fruit fresh from the orchards. Captions critics, therefore, who speak neither in sympathy with the objects of the association nor knowledge of the matter in question, display more shrewdness than manliness in withholding their names when expressing their views in the public print.

I here append a letter received from Mr. A. McD. Allan, for years the president of the Ontario Fruit Growers' Association, who had charge of the Canadian fruit exhibit at the Colonial Exhibition in London, Eng., who practically established the Canadian apple trade in England, who is an authority in pomology throughout America, and who was instrumental in organising this association.

[Unfortunately, Mr. Allen's letter has been mislaid. Mr. Allen, however, speaks in the strongest possible way of the British Columbia fruit as shown at Toronto, which he refers to as an "object lesson" of great interest to him. Many varieties, he says, seem to improve in British Columbia, not only in size and color, but in flavor. Our cherries, in his opinion, are equal to the best German cherries. Mr. Allen expresses surprise that any person could speak in any sense disparagingly of the British Columbia exhibit, either as to quality or arrangement. He spent some time in the British Columbia court, which to him was the most interesting feature of the whole exhibit.—Ed.]

As the gravamen of the objections reported related to the poor quality of the fruit exhibited, I feel justified in referring to the matter as fully as I have, and the above letter is only one of about a dozen similar which I have received. It is a matter, too, affecting the credit of the province, because if the fruit was a disgrace to British Columbia, the onus must be on a number of our representative fruit growers who contributed the specimens, and on the province and not on the association. I know no better way of advertising the province than that of showing its fruit capabilities, because in no way has it more fertile resources. To the average man with average capital, ability and intelligence, fruit growing offers more inducements than any other calling, and I believe, with all our wealth of minerals, fish and timber, there is more gold, industry and ultimate and permanent prosperity lying dormant in the . possibilities of horticulture than any of those named. It is, too, one of those industries into which competition and the multiplication of values enter beneficially to the whole. It is only, and it is the experience of all fruit countries, when a surplus of products is created, when new markets must be discovered and gained, that success is certain. When British Columbia can ship by the carload, fresh and preserved fruits to the Northwest and to eastern Canada, and shiploads, as she does salmon and lumber, that fruit growing will be placed on a permanent and paying basis. Until Canada found a market for apples in England, her orchards were encumberances rather than acquisitions. Rates cannot be obtained from carrying companies that will make it pay, until carloads can be made up. Fruit trains go out of California weekly, and daily, it may be, at certain seasons, and fruits are distributed from such competing points as Chicago, all through the east, and that is because there is a surplus of fruit to ship that must be got rid of, and though the prices are such that British Columbia growers would not deign to accept, by the mere plenty which abounds, it pays. Ontario growers tell me that grapes at a cent a pound pay them. Fruit is sold in California as low as $\frac{1}{2}$ cent a pound, and makes dividends. Carloads of California fruit went into Winnipeg weekly last summer. That is our market by all manner of rights, but dealers there would be greatly disappointed if they looked for even one carload in a season from British Columbia. Of course, we all understand that this is a new province and that we must creep before we walk. Still, I do not think the progress has been made that should have been. There is no reason why British Columbia, with similar resources and horticultural conditions, should not stand in the same relation to Canada that California does to the United States, that is in fruits clearly within her capabilities.

There are several reasons for the backwardness characteristic of this province. One is, that owing to so much of the best lands being locked up in the hands of speculators, the class of settlers that we most need for development has not been attracted. The available lands have been made too high. Another is, that the prices of produce, heretofore with the facilities for making a living so favorable, have rendered it unnecessary to put forth earnest efforts to succeed. There is such a thing as being too well off. The old adage has it that "necessity is the mother of invention." As a matter of fact, there is no place on this continent where greater care and labor are necessary to produce good results than in British Columbia. As we know, a great deal of hap-hazard work has been done, and orchards planted without reference to subsequent cultivation, or the varieties required. Reckless and irresponsible fruit tree agents have filled the province with trees of all kinds and varieties, half of them the very antithesis of their representations, and as a result there are many orchards in bearing that ought to be very remunerative, which have not enough of any one good variety to pay, or the varieties are totally unsuited. Then, if I may be pardoned for broaching on that subject again, what fruit is good is shipped in a manner which does not take the market, with the result that it is lower in prices and less preferred than Oregon and eastern fruit that has been carried long distances, whereas, being fresh from the orchard, it should command first place. Here I more particularly refer to apples, plums, pears and even cherries. Go to any fruit store and examine two boxes of any kind, one British Columbia and the other imported. The one box to start with, has no pretensions to neatness, and two or three varieties of varying sizes are thrown in pell-mell. The other may be in the average, inferior fruit, but the box is light and neat, there is only one variety, one apple is the measure of all the rest, and when it is opened the arrangement is like balls in a counting frame. A customer does not even stop to think which he will choose. It may be a trick of the trade, but it is a trick that pays, and one, however conservative we are, we must learn to make fruit growing pay. In saying this, it is not to appear critical or air any superior wisdom. It is the truth, as every fruit dealer knows can testify.

To remedy this, it is necessary to start over again, and begin on first principles. There are three things to do: First choose the varieties the market demands, and for which the province is best suited; second, to cultivate with a view to the best results; third, to systematize the sale of orchard products. Another element has unexpectedly entered to complicate the problem. A number of canneries have suddenly sprung into existence, and a little prematurely, it would seem, in view of the abilities of the province to supply them. Cannery men are faced with several unlooked for difficulties. Fruit is not plentiful enough, and consequently not cheap enough to afford a dividend on their operations; and again they cannot get the right varieties for canning. Growing fruit for canneries is quite another thing to growing it for the fruit dealer. For instance, certain varieties of fruits, plums, cherries, pears, and so on, may sell well in the market, but are no, or little, good for canning purposes. The question is, what varieties should be grown.

To solve these several problems there is but one reasonable, common sense way. Local experience is not sufficient to tell us what varieties are best suited to our climate and our market. Nobody knows, because nobody has lived long enough in the business here to find out. Canning is a new business here, and therefore most of us are in the dark as to its requiremedts. To find out we must go where these problems have already been solved. We must look to Oregon and California. Then the climatological and other conditions are very similar. With isothermal modifications the whole Pacific coast is similar in its biology. It is a reasonable assumption, therefore, that what will succeed in Oregon and California will have fair prospects of succeeding in British Columbia. The commercial aspect of fruit growing is very much the same here as there.

This is a day of commissions. There are mining commissions, boodling commissions, civil service commissions, commissions to investigate irregularities in municipal affairs, fishery commissions, and what not. If a man, or two or three men, go wrong in office, and a lot of money goes with them it costs the country as much more to find out where it has gone to. The farmer bears the greater brunt of all this, and it is about time the farmer and fruit-grower had a commission too. I would suggest and recommend to this association that the government of British Columbia be memorialized to appoint a commission of two or three practical men, who know what is wanted, not office seekers or political spongers, to go down the coast as far as Southern California, study the whole question thoroughly from root to branch, including the minutest details of varieties, planting, cultivation, canning, selling, and so on, and present a concise report for publication and distribution to every farmer in the province. This report might incidentally include hop raising, which is not generally understood, or, in fact, not at all in British Columbia ; poultry raising and one or two other matters of importance that might come easily within the notice of said commissioners. More good would result from this than all the commissions and pretensions and awe-inspiring investigations that this country has ever suffered. Gentlemen, these are some of the impressions I have formed east as well as at home about British Columbia fruit, and if my cogitations have been productive of a single idea worth resoluting upon, I shall be fully repaid for the wear and tear of mental tissue. Somebody or other said, "be sure you are right, and then go ahead." Grant said, that the way to resume was to resume, and I shall resume my seat by remarking that the way to do something is to do it. If the British Columbia Fruit Growers' Association is to accomplish the mission for which it was allegedly brought into existence, the members want to do more than to discuss resolutions and read papers, which only see light again in the annual report, but are like the unproductive seed in the parable of the sower. There is, without doubt, a lot to do, and a wide field for usefulness. To use a vulgar Americanism, the association should walk into that field with both feet.

CANNING AND PRESERVING FRUIT.

PAPER BY MR. MORRIS, OF ORELL & MORRIS, VICTORIA.

Nearly all the ills that man is heir to find their antidote in the variety of fruits culled from every part of the globe. No wonder we should read in the Old Book, "My fruit is better than gold, yea, than much fine gold." The mention of fruit never fails to inspire thoughts of the pleasantest kind. They delight the palate, they please the eye, and in contemplation of their artistic and classic form, hue and fragrance, who has not with their pretty wiles and persuasions been intoxicated with their lucious nectar. Very rarely do men refuse fruit, for here nature has concentrated her richest powers. Brought to perfection under the genial influence of sunshine, they are themselves like sunbeams of Heaven, and ask from us simply their reception and enjoyment. The abundance which nature supplies has been with no niggard hand, and happy the people whose climate permits her to plant, to tend and foster the many kinds that are suitable to their country.

You will have noticed on the agenda paper, that the subject down is on "Preserving." Now, as we have experienced some little difficulty in procuring the right kinds of fruit, and as we have frequently been asked by farmers and others the kinds to grow, you will perhaps pardon me if, for a few moments I, give a sketch of what I think will suit the manufacturers or home preservers. Fruit culture is no longer a hap-hazard work, but it is now conducted upon scientific principles, and as the best kinds of fruits are obtainable, there is no excuse for inferior trees being planted. Now, as our object is to treat of the varieties that may be successfully grown in British Columbia, we will begin with apples, and without entering into their origin and structure we may say that they have been carried to all parts of the world, but that hot countries are not the most favorable to their growth. It does fairly well in New Zealand, and I saw in January and February of last year apples that looked almost like peaches, and these were selling at 12 and 14 cents per lb. But no country in the world is more favorable to the growth of apples than the continent of America, that is, Canada and some parts of the States, and from what I have seen at your local exhibitions, this province may claim to grow some of the largest apples the world has seen. Their quality may not be as good, and their productiveness as great as some we know. This may be the result of not knowing, in many cases, the right kind to plant, hence, this association must be an enormous boon to the province and worthy of every support. At an exhibition held some time ago in England there were placed upon the tables no less than ten thousand dishes of apples, representing two thousand and twenty varieties, of which the judges allowed 1,554 to be distinct, and with a view to which was the best kind to grow, a poll was taken, when the following stood at the top of the tree : In the *southern counties*, Cox's Orange, King of Pippins, Ribston Pippin, Blenheim Orange, Kerry Pippin ; *eastern counties*, Cox's Orange, Blenheim Orange, Kerry Pippin, Irish Pippin ; *midland counties*, Cox's Orange, King of Pippins, Ribston Pippin, Kerry Pippin. It will be seen that the King of Pippins was Cox's Orange. This tree is noted for its splendid bearing qualities, and if planted in this country would do well ; so would the Keswick Codling and Lord Suffield, and of all varieties none would be more profitable to the farmer than the celebrated Baldwin. It is a splendid keeper and its culinary qualities make it a general favorite. In passing through Oregon and California recently, I noticed that this tree was very largely planted and is being sent over here in large quantities. I would like to suggest here that if the farmers would go to a little more trouble in grading and packing their apples, that every apple should be plucked from the tree and carefully packed in rows in the box. We have much to learn from the States and New Zealand in this respect. Living in the neighborhood of Manchester, Eng., I frequently went to Shudhill market, perhaps the largest wholesale and retail market in the world, and in conversation with the largest importers, was told that those farmers who graded and packed their apples in rows and wrapped them in tissue paper, and took every care, could always fetch the largest price and sell the best. Now, here is a sample of what was brought to our preserve factory at Victoria, and Mr. Okell, my partner, will vouch for the statement. Apples have been sent to us by the farmers, small, little scrubs, and different kinds mixed, and even potatoes, and these have been put into boxes, cut out in the rough, and have weighed 25 pounds. These have been what is called 50-lb. boxes. One word more and we will pass on, but it would be a pity not to name the pretty little fruit, the Siberian crab or cherry apple. It is one of those that seem to take a position between the wild and cultivated, but though called a crab, it is quite distinct from the wild apple. It is rather sharp, but inviting, when made into conserves. I am not sure but that the farmers are neglecting to plant this tree. Being wishful to send over to England last Summer, with our other goods, we found them scarce. Now, while Canada and the States head the list as apple growing countries, France, Belgium and the Channel Islands produce the largest pears. I have seen some that have been exhibited in this country, certainly very fine, but for flavor and dimensions you are at present behind. There is room tor improvement, and with a climate such as we possess, it is only a question of time. Among those raised in England, none excel that beautiful lemon, yellow, with blush on the sunward side, named Lucy Greive; Knight's Monarch, sugary and perfumed; River's Beacon, bright and handsome, and for stewing, and turning a rich crimson is not to be beaten; and never forget to plant the Jargonelle and Marre Louise. But do not expect pears of the finest quality and flavor where the soil is wet, cold and clayey. The early history of the plum is rather remote and complicated, but for the sake of convenience we will divide them into three distinct and typical forms : The sloe, sloe thorn and black thorn; secondly, the bullace (*prunis institia*); and thirdly, which from its appearance, would indicate it to be the source of the garden plums, called *prunus domestica*. It is usual for botanists to call all these by the same name, *prunus domestica*. Now, in England, unquestionably the most valuable of all varieties is the Damson. It is hardy, easily cultivated and yields large crops. There are several varieties, but the one that stands without a rival is the Farleigh. The fruit is small, but is produced in abundant clusters and is unsurpassed for preserving. Now, why have not the farmers in this splendid district planted this tree in great quantities? I notice you can grow the Golden Egg plum to perfection, and although I have an intimate knowledge of the fruits of Oregon and California, I have seen nothing to surpass what can be produced here in the Golden Egg, Washington and Victoria, and I argue from this that the French, Italian and German prunes, which are produced in such abundance in Washington and Oregon that they have to ship thousands of boxes east after their own wants are supplied, can surely be grown here. I am told that you are feeding your cattle or pigs with certain kinds. There is no need for this, for if you will grow the right kinds, and come to the manufacturers, we will tell you how to turn them into dollars. Another favorite fruit that might be grown in greater quantities is the apricot, loving, as it does, the moisture of the sea, planted in sunny and protected positions or between apple trees, I think, with a climate such as we have, it ought to receive greater attention. Among the various small fruits, I would name only those that will be most profitable to the growers. Now, it may not be generally known, but from the information I have gleaned, nearly all the preserves made from small fruits have been coming from England or the east, and British Columbia, with a climate second to none for the growth of such, is not producing what she ought, and what are grown are fetching splendid prices, as the following will show. A farmer told me about two months ago, that out of one acre of land, after all expenses were paid, that he cleared $419, clear profit. This was in strawberries. Now, we are prepared, and I dare say other manufacturers are prepared also, to take tons of these. The same may be said of raspberries, for jam made from this is, without question, the most delightfully aromatic that can be conceived. And of the blackberries, you can grow them such as no other country can surpass, either for size or quality. I am under the impression that we are lacking in gooseberries, and here Great Britain bears away the palm. The best way to grow them is, unquestionably, upon trellices, the plants then require little space, are easily pruned, and the summer growth cleared out of the way, the wood gets better matured and heavier crops are the result. As to the best kinds to grow, tastes vary. Of the red, white, yellow and green, the yellow is acknowledged to be the richest and most vinous in flavor. With reference to currants, red white and black, the specimens I have seen, are not up to the mark. The black currants delight in a rich, strong soil, and stand deservedly high and as a medicinal conserve, being soothing, tonic and stimulant, and will well repay all who have land to grow them.

I propose now to give some of the principles on which fruit may be preserved. Having had considerable experience, 1 may lay claim to know some-something, however little, of this art, for it is an art, and if conducted on scientific principles, with minds open to receive fresh instruction, the benefit will be for the welfare of mankind. To carry out the best mode of preserving, it must be done on a large scale, and a thorough and practical knowledge of the degrees of sugar boiling is necessary. The number of these degrees vary, but the object of this paper is to give a brief and clear idea, to instruct, and not to confuse, so I will call the first degree the smooth or 215 degree by the thermometer, and as an example, we will take 12 pounds of sugar, crystal, to 3 pints of water and boil this for five minutes. Dip in a tea spoon and draw between the finger and thumb, and if it feels smooth, this is the degree called the smooth and is used for crystallizing liquors and various other goods. The second is the thread or 230 degrees of the thermometer. Now, in the course of a few minutes the sugar passes into this degree. If you try the spoon again, close your finger and thumb and gently part them, you will perceive a thread-like appearance. It has now passed into this stage and is used for syrups and bon bons. The third may be called the blow or feather, and is 240 degrees. Now, if you were to dip in a skimmer with holes in, into the pan and draw it out quickly, and then blow very hard through it you will perceive bladders or feathery particles pass away, and this stage is used .for candying peel, fruit and so on. Now, in order to be a good preserve maker, it is necessary to have an intimate knowledge of the degrees of sugar boiling, so as to prevent fermentation, and thus enable them to be kept for years. Jams and marmalades originally were used to convey one and the same meaning, but are now understood to mean different processes. The term marmalade is now applied to those fruits that are of a mucilangus nature, such as oranges and lemons, while the term jam has reference to those of a soft nature and very readily converted into pulp with or without the aid of heat. Now, taking this as a basis or guide, you see jams and marmalades may be made from all fruits, always considering that the fruit must be of a firm, dry nature, and now that sugar is so much cheaper than it was, it is like spoiling the ship for the sake of five cents of tar, where, from motives of economy, less quantities of sugar are used than ought to be. Now, it has sometimes been thought that fruit that was wet would not preserve, but such is not the case, for if placed in the pan and boiled before the sugar is added, evaporation takes place and the water is excluded. There are many people think that fruit in all its stages may be preserved, but such is not the case, and many years ago I read of the different periods of maturity that fruit undergoes. I understand it to be four kinds, and may briefly be described as : First, maturity of vegetation, that is when the fruit has gone through the vegetable process of ripening and looks ready to fall from the tree. The second is the maturity of honeyfication, and this consists in the ripeness and flavor which fruits of all kinds acquire if plucked a few days before arriving at their first maturity. The third stage is that of expectation, or that degree which it assumes, which, although ripe enough to drop off the tree, are even then hard or sour, such as many pears or apples, which improve after keeping. The fourth degree of maturity may be described as artificial, and is nothing more than the change produced by cooking. Now, for preserving fruits whole, as well as making them into jams, the fruits must be taken at the right time or state to keep the aroma and nutritous qualities of the various kinds, and those who have studied this question of preserving the fruits and retaining the bloom, the flesh and all the properties of the many kinds which they handle, are benefactors of their race. It has been said that ordinary jam fruit and sugar which have been boiled together, keep much better if the jars into which the jam is poured be tied up while hot. If the jam is allowed to cool before being fastened up, little germs will fall upon it from the air and will soon fall to work to decompose the fruit, but if fastened up while hot, the germs which are floating in it will be scalded. I do not attach much importance to it, neither to the method used by some, of dipping the paper with which you cover the tops, in spirits or brandy, for when the spirit has evaporated, as it soon will, it leaves the paper hard and dry, and very often brings with it the preserve. The method I would recommend is to cut the paper the proper size and dip it into a little salad or olive oil, and if the jar is hermetically sealed, it will keep for years if properly boiled. I would advise that they should be kept in a cool, dry current of air.

I think it is only right to say that under certain set conditions and circumstances, jams may be boiled to a set time, but no instruction can be given without knowing the kind of fruit used, for you will find that various fruits require different treatments and the quantity and sizes of jars used, for instance, a large quantity takes a longer time to get to the boil than a smaller quantity, and time must also be allowed for evaporation. Now, if you boil the preserve until it jellies when put out on a plate, this may be taken as a safe guide. Now, it may be asked what do you think of putting preserves in tin. And here I may be treading upon delicate ground, for many manufacturers, and good manufacturers too, do put jam into tin. I do not blame them, but I may venture to say, that in my judgment, it is not the wisest and best mode of packing, and if the general public will insist upon having them in glass or crockery, the manufacturers will only be too happy to supply them. I think it will be readily granted that it is almost impossible to keep fruits and jams with acid juices in tins for long without the acid acting more or less upon the tin, and almost stripping it from the iron. We have heard over and over again that metallic impurity in the shape of tin has caused serious illness. Acid fruits, then, should never be preserved in anything but glass or porcelain vessels. I think the day is coming in British Columbia when we who have every facility for manufacturing glass and crockery, such as no country can heat, will have nothing but the very best mode of packing. I wish I might say the same with reference to having genuine jams, for many of the raspberry and strawberry jams, etc., derive their claim to this solely from the presence of a small percentage of the genuine article. Chemical fruit essences added to apple stock, colored with aniline and other dyes, with sufficient dried tomato and other seeds, give them the natural appearance. Now, how can the real jam be sold to pay the cost of production, the sugar and packages, etc., excepting by charging a fair price? No wonder that ladies wish to preserve their own, yet I would not be misunderstood, for if these goods be put up, that is, genuine fruit and granulated sugar in, in small quantities, they can not be so fine, nor the flavor be kept as when manufactured in large quantities in properly constructed pans.

Now, with reference to canned or bottled whole fruits. I think these stand pre-eminent, for by this mode of packing, you retain the medicinal qualities of the fruit. An all-wise Providence has provided fruit suitable to the preservation of our health, and are designed to appear at the very time that our bodies require their renovating influences. That considerable trouble has to be taken, one single illustration may be given. Take fine peaches, prick them with a needle, throw them into cold water and stand a little while, then let the water boil up to soften them, take them out with a ladle, put them into more cold water, when cold drain them and arrange them in an earthen pan, then cover them with syrup boiled to a thread, next day draw off the syrup, boil it a little higher, adding more syrup, keep them in this three days; repeat the same process: fourth day drain them and boil the syrup more; put it over the fruit and just boil them up in it and put them in jars for use. Some fruits require as many as six or seven syrups, and are of much trouble and no little expense. I will now bring my remarks to a close by giving a *modus operandi* of preserving fruits in a crystallized or glazed form, and I think is not only interesting but one of considerable attraction, and well worthy of a place in this paper and of your association. The process is quite simple and consists firstly, in extracting the juice from the fruit operated upon. The next is to replace the juice with sugar syrup, and when this hardens, which it will do, prevents the fruit from decaying, and at the same time keep the perfect form of the fruit. First, very great care is required in selecting the fruit. It must be all of one size as near as possible, all of the same ripeness. The stage at which it is selected is of vital importance. Say that degree of ripeness that is best suitable for canning. The various fruits are pitted and now are placed, say in a basket, and dipped into boiling water. This is done to extract the juice. Now, the length of time they stop in the water is of importance, for if the juices be not extracted, the fruit will not absorb the sugar, and if it remains in the water too long it will become soft. Let it now cool and sort again as to softness. The syrup must be about 70 degrees of the taccharometer. After this the fruit is placed into dishes or pans and the syrup poured over and allowed to remain about a week. It now requires every attention as fermentation will now begin, and both the fruit and the syrup must be brought to the boil and this will check it for a little time, but the process must be repeated for five or six weeks.

PLUMS AND PRUNES.

PAPER BY JOHN KIRKLAND, LADNER'S.

Mr. President and Gentlemen,

The favorable reputation which our province has already acquired for the size and quality of its plums and prunes, is a sufficient guarantee that our climate and soil is capable of producing this class of fruit in unlimited quantity and in the highest state of perfection. Such being the case, let us confidently hope that in the near future the cultivation of these fruits as staple articles of commerce will be commensurate with the natural advantages we possess for their production, and that concurrently with other branches of fruit culture, this branch may become one of the leading industries of our province.

Success in the culture of these fruits may be achieved under varying conditions of soil, situation or surroundings, but, as in all fruit culture, the best success can only be attained by the adoption of an efficient system of drainage and a thorough cultivation of the ground, both before and after the trees have been planted.

Upon our delta lands the vigorous growth of young wood necessitates an heroic application of the pruning knife annually to prevent the splitting of the trees under the weight of their superabundance of fruit.

My own plum orchard is composed in part of Peach, Bradshaws, Eggs (red and yellow), Deearn's Purple, Jefferson, the Gages and others with whose names I am not familiar, and of prunes, the French and German, the Silver, the Italian, the Hungarian and the English.

Of the varieties above mentioned the Peach plum, among the earlier sorts, is incomparably the best, being a plentiful cropper, of first-class quality, and being of medium but even size, handsome and attractive in color, it is a welcomed variety in every market. My experience, nevertheless, has proved the trees to be very liable to injury by the bursting of their bark in the early spring, which has a very injurious effect on their growth, and in too many cases results in ultimate death. How far this trouble is the result of being grafted upon peach stocks I do not presume to say, never myself having taken the trouble to justify the suspicion by careful comparison with trees differently grafted; therefore, I leave the problem for experts to solve. One of the next to ripen is the Bradshaw—a tree of a robust habit and vigorous growth, a capital bearer of large-sized, wine-colored fruit, and, though the flesh is somewhat coarse in texture, is a popular variety for general use. For later varieties none have given more satisfactory results than the Egg plums, both yellow and red. Both are of good quality, their large size and color being pleasing to the eye. They are never a drug in the market, but invariably command the highest price the market can afford. Many other kinds of plums might be mentioned, which are worthy of equal commendation, did space permit.

Of prunes, all the varieties above named I have found well suited to our soil and climate and consider them all worthy of cultivation.

And now let me, as an amateur fruit grower, say, in conclusion, that while I think British Columbia is destined to become the greatest fruit-producing province in the Dominion by virtue of the suitability of its climate for the greater number of semi-tropical fruits, as well as by its commercial position, I am also convinced that the best financial success to be achieved in fruit growing will be attained by the man who grows none but the choicest varieties which are to be obtained in the branch in which he may be engaged, and whose constant aim is to produce none but such as shall always command the brand of an A 1 quality in the market.

A PLEA FOR OUR NATIVE FLOWERING SHRUBS.

PAPER BY T. WILSON, HARRISON RIVER.

At the last general meeting of the Fruit Growers' Association, I spoke of some of the native fruits, and, since then, it has occurred to me that a few words about the flowering shrubs might not be amiss. It is surprising how little attention has been paid to them in ornamenting our places. "Birds from far away have fine feathers," is an old proverb, and I think it aptly applies in this case. Hundreds of dollars are spent annually to bring in ornamental trees and shrubs from other countries, while those growing at our own doors are left unnoticed. Don't think, for an instant, that I disparage any efforts made in this direction; on the contrary, I am an enthusiast in bringing in anything new, but I think that a place ought to be found for some of those nearer home, more especially as many of them improve greatly under cultivation.

As this is not a nurseryman's descriptive catalogue, I will not weary you with any long details, but only mention a few which will well repay cultivation in the pleasure to be derived from their fine appearance.

The first that I will notice is the well known Oregon Grape *(Berberis Aqua folium)*. The leaves are always handsome, very much resembling holly, and when the plants are crowned with their spike of bright yellow flowers, which, later on, are succeeded by bunches of blue grape-like berries, they are truly ornamental anywhere. I have some of them 8 feet high.

Flowering about the same time is another grand flowering shrub, the red flowering currant *(Ribes Sanguineum)*. This is common enough anywhere, and will succeed in the most stony ground.

There is a cream-colored variety which is sometimes met with. Among the Spireas there are three which deserve notice. The first, Spirea Aruncus, sometimes named Goat's Beard, cannot be called a shrub, as it dies down in the winter, but with its grand racemes of flowers it is a conspicuous object growing along the line of the C.P.R. The flowers are sometimes eighteen inches in length.

I don't know that I dare mention the next—S. Douglasii—as it is so difficult to clear and eradicate that hardly any one will have a good word to say of the *Hardack*, still, like many other weeds, it is beautiful in its place.

The third Spirea is Arœfolia, which sometimes attains to the size of a small tree, and its spikes of cream-colored flowers have the appearance of bunches of feathers.

Some of the raspberries might well be classed among the ornamental flowering shrubs, more particularly the salmonberry *(Rubus spectabilis)*. Not being like others of the rasps, it does not die down in winter, and, consequently, can be trained to any height. It is the earliest flowering of the genus, and as it flowers and fruits abundantly, the effect is kept up for a long time.

I think we have only one thorn indigenous to this part, viz.; Cratægus Douglasii. It is too well known to need more mention.

The western juneberry *(Amelankier alnifolia)* certainly deserves a place, not only for its beautiful snow-white flowers, but for its delicious fruit.

The Mock orange *(Philadelphus Lewisii)* grows with great luxuriance and certainly improves with cultivation.

Another grand looking tree is the western flowering Dogwood (*Comus Nuttallii*). When this is in bloom it is truly magnificent. I have measured some of the flowers four and a half inches across. I noticed some trees that flowered twice during the past season—in May, and again in October.

Among others that may well be cultivated are the high bush cranberry, the scarlet flowering honeysuckle, and, for training over rock work, the *Arctostaphyllos Alpina*, or Alpine bearberry. This is one of the most delicate flowering things we have of the heath order, and another, the Gaultheria Shaton, is also very handsome. The Labrador Tea (*Ledum latifolia*) is also worthy of a little space.

Now, although we have not exhausted the list by any means, the above is quite a variety to choose from, and as they are within reach of most of us, we ought to have enough to make our places highly attractive.

SOME FACTS ABOUT BEES.

BY R. L. CODD, HATZIC.

Mr. President and Gentlemen:

In preparing this paper to read before you, I would say that it is with a feeling of uncertainty as to whether it will prove interesting, alike to those of your members who keep bees, as well as to those who prefer to have the bees just a little way off but have no objection to the honey.

I will begin by giving some quotations from a paper on "Bees as fertilizers," read at an agricultural meeting in the States, by Prof. A. J. Cook, of the Michigan State Agricultural College, whose name, I daresay, is familiar to the most of you, as a writer on all agricultural topics, and he is familiar to the bee-keeping fraternity as a scientific investigator of the nature and habits of the honey bee. In speaking of the value of bees as fertilizers in the early spring before flies and other insects are numerous enough to be of value in that line he says: "By actual count in time of fruit bloom, I have found the bees twenty to one of all other insects upon the flowers; and on cool days, which are very common at this early season, I have known hundreds of bees on the fruit blossoms, while I could not find a single other insect. Thus we see that the honey bees are exceedingly important in the economy of vegetable growth and fruitage, especially of all such plants as blossom early in the season." In speaking again of how important the bees are in the pollenization of plants, he says: "To determine this point I tried many experiments last spring. I counted the blossoms on each of two branches, or plants, of apple, pear, cherry, strawberry, raspberry and clover. One of these in case of each fruit, or each experiment, was surrounded by cheese cloth just before the blossoms opened and kept covered till the blossoms fell off. The apple, pear and cherry were covered May the 4th, and uncovered May the 19th and 25th. The number of blossoms considered varied from 32, the smallest number, to 300, the largest. The trees were examined June the 11th to see what number of the fruit had set. The per cent. of blossoms which developed on the covered trees was a little over two, while almost twenty per cent. of the uncovered blossoms had developed, Of the pears, not one of the covered blossoms developed, while five per cent. of the uncovered developed fruit. Of the cherries, three per cent. only of the covered developed, while forty per cent. of the uncovered set their fruit. The strawberries were covered May the 18th, and uncovered June the 16th. The number of blossoms of each experiment varied from 60, least, to 212 in the greatest. In these cases a box covered with cheese cloth, surrounded the plants. The plants were examined June the 22nd. Eleven per cont. of the covered blossoms and seventeen per cent. of the uncovered had developed. To show the details, in one case 60 blossoms were considered, nine of which in the covered lot, and 27 in the uncovered had developed. That is, three times as many flowers had set in the uncovered as in the covered. In another case of 212 blossoms the fruit numbered 80 and 104. In a case of 123 blossoms, the number of fruit was 20 and 36." These experiments agree with similar ones of former years, in seeming to show that strawberries are less affected than other fruit by the exclusion of insect visits. The raspberry canes were covered with cheese cloth May the 30th, and uncovered July 6th. In every case but one the canes seem to have been injured by the covers, and so the results were not considered. In the exceptional case, 184 blossoms were considered ; 93 blossoms developed on the covered canes and 160 on the uncovered. In every case the fruit on the covered twigs was inferior. It might be thought that the simple presence of the covers was prejudicial ; though this could not be a very important matter, as blossoms covered after the bees had visited them showed no injury. Thus we see that in all our fruits—strawberries the least—the free visits of insects during the period of blooming is absolutely essential to a full, or even a fair crop. In many cases the covered blossoms all failed to develop. We also see that where fruitage does occur, there seems a lack, as the fruit lacks vigor. The free and ample cross fertilization seems to be requisite, not only for a crop, but for a perfect development and maximum vigor." "Our experiments with clover were tried with both the white and the alsike. While the uncovered heads were full of seeds, the covered ones were entirely seedless. This fully explains the common experience of farmers with these plants." "Having the law of the necessity of insects to accomplish this function so well demonstrated, it might be asked, 'Why do we have any fruit in case the blossoms are covered?' This seeming exception may be no exception. Indeed, this may come from the fact that *all* insects are not excluded. Very small insects, like the thrips and various forms of the jassidal, which we know are often attracted to flowers, either by the pollen or nectar, would be concealed about the plants, and, from their small size might gain access even after the covers were adjusted. These would be sufficient to secure partial fertilization, and very likely are the cause of the meagre crop which, in a few cases, we secured, even on the covered twigs." "In case of strawberries, our experiments this year, like some previously tried, seemed to show that the presence of insects, though important to a maximum production, are not necessary as in the case of nearly all other fruits, but we can still affirm in the case of the strawberry, that the free visits of insects serve to much enlarge the production of fruit. Thus we see that our horticulturists and farmers alike with the apiarist are dependent for the best prosperity on the presence and well being of the bees."

It would seem by this that the bees are really the natural agents for spreading pollen, and they are the only insects that appear to do the work thoroughly. To be convinced of this, we need only to watch the bee at work gathering pollen, when she will be seen to not only scratch the pollen up by means of her front feet, but she purposely rubs the under side of her body against the pollen mass ; she then rises into the air and conveys some moisten-ed pollen from her tongue to the pollen baskets on her hind legs, and adds some of the dry material from the hairs of her body, when the operation is repeated till a full load is secured.

The habits of the bee are a most wonderful and interesting study. We will consider some of the peculiarities of the queen bee first, or as she is more properly called, the mother bee, for she does not exercise authority over the other inmates of the hive, but is subject more or less to their wishes. If we open up a hive of bees on some nice warm day, and very quietly take out the comb the queen is on, so as not to disturb her too much, she will presently resume her duty of egg laying, while round about her will be seen a number of young bees (not many days hatched), standing with their heads towards her, offering her food, which she partakes of whenever hungry, and to all appearances she has a good appetite, but such might be expected, seeing that she lays from 1,000 to 3,000 eggs a day during the honey season. This matter of feeding the queen during the season of breeding seems to be done for the economy of time, for at times when she is not laying she has to get her own food from the cells like the other bees in the hive. It will also be noticed that during times of scarcity of honey very few eggs will be laid. Whether this is the queen's doing or not is hard to say, but I think that as her time is spent on the empty combs away from where the honey is being stored, it is more likely to be the workers that govern egg laying, by witholding the amount of food given to the queen, which is of a special form, being composed of partly digested pollen which is easy of digestion and goes rapidly to the formation of eggs, or possibly there is a means of communication between the members of the bee hive family. That they can hear is admitted by all scientific men, but so far they have failed to locate the organs of hearing for a certainty. It is supposed they are located in the antemol, those horn-like appendages on the front of the bee's head, which, when subjected to a high magnifying power, present a very complicated appearance. That they are the means of touch and smell has been established without a doubt. The queen is capable of laying two kinds of eggs, i. e., fertilized eggs, which produce workers, and unfertilized eggs, which produce drones ; and here is a most wonderful thing. After the queen is mated, and that only takes place once in her lifetime before egg laying commences, she is then capable of laying eggs as above at her will. The fertilizing fluid is contained in a sac for the purpose, and according to her will she fertilizes the eggs or not at the time of laying. So you see the mating of the queen affects the workers and queen progeny only, for the unfertilized eggs (those laid to produce drones,) do not partake of the male fluid with which the queen fertilizes the eggs intended to produce workers; this has been proved by microscopical examinations, but perhaps the surest proof is the following: If a pure Italian queen mates with a black drone, her worker bees will show the characteristics of both races, while the drones she produces will be like herself, pure Italian, so you see the drone has no father, but is purely the son of his mother, for a queen can lay drone eggs if she never meets the drone in her life, but not worker eggs. Another remarkable thing is that the worker eggs are undeveloped females, which difference between them and the queen herself being a fully developed female, is caused entirely by the food administered to them in their earliest stage by the nurse bees. The egg that produces a worker will likewise produce a queen, there being no difference in the egg, but in the feed given to the young bee. This has been found out by analysis. Three days after the egg has been laid, it hatches into a tiny worm, properly known as a larva. In case a queen is desired from this larva, it is fed most liberally for five days on a prepared food of partly digested pollen, when the cell is then sealed over and the queen hatches in seven or eight days thereafter. On the other hand, if a worker bee is desired from this same larva, it is fed for three days only on this partly digested pollen, when it is then weaned from that and fed sparingly for five days more on undigested pollen and honey, at the end of which time it is sealed over, and thirteen days after comes forth as a worker bee. It has been found if the worker larva is fed more than three days on the partly digested pollen, that the ovaries begin to develop rapidly, thereby causing the production of a perfect female or queen bee. I will close by giving the management of bees during the different seasons of the year.

SPRING MANAGEMENT.

When warm weather comes for good, it is as well to open up each hive and see that it contains a laying queen, to which the presence of brood will attest, if you do not happen to see the queen herself. All dead bees should be removed from inside the hives, and the entrance contracted to one inch of space, more or less, according to size of the colony, to enable them to keep out robber bees which are apt to give trouble at this season. They should also be supplied with stores if short.

SUMMER MANAGEMENT.

As soon as the bees are noticed to lengthen the ends of the cells at the tops of the combs, top stories containing sections, or extracting combs, may be put on, provided the body of the hive is pretty well filled with bees. As soon as there are thirty-four finished, raise up the first storey and place an empty one underneath it, or the sections in the first storey can be removed as fast as completed, or in case of extracted honey, extract the honey from the first storey as soon as half sealed one, and return combs to be filled again, always being careful to keep the bees provided with plenty of room to work in, and here I would say comb honey is not a profitable crop to raise in this country, for two reasons. First, the nights are too cool, and entirely too cool after the middle of July for the bees to secrete wax to advantage, for unless the colony is exceptionally strong in numbers, the bees will leave the sections at night and cluster down below the brood, and at night is when comb building should go on most rapidly. Secondly, the difference in price between comb and extracted honey is not sufficient to warrant the production to any extent of the former.

FALL MANAGEMENT.

About the middle of September (in my locality) top storeys may be taken off for good, and if hy the first of October the lower part of the hive is not well filled with honey, they should be fed back sufficient to give them at least 25 or 30 pounds of stores.

WINTER MANAGEMENT.

As soon as cold or frosty nights come, the hives should be gone over and the old gummy cotton covers removed and clean ones put on, underneath which place three one inch sticks, crosswise of the frames, so as to allow the bees a passage way over the top of the frames ; then put on the top storeys and fill up to within an inch of the top with dry chaff, old clothes, or better, thoroughly dried rotten wood, preferably that from fir or cedar. If the packing gets damp, remove the cover of the hive for five days and let the sunshine in.

HOP CULTURE.

PAPER BY JOHN L. BROE, SHORTREED.

I am pleased with the profits on hops. I have raised four crops of hops, and although my land has not been drained properly, I have raised an average of nearly 1200 lbs. per acre, and have obtained an average price for same of 24 cents per pound. The total cost of raising hops is about 6 cents per pound, which leaves me a net profit of 15 cents per pound, or $180 per acre per year.

On a favorable location and soil, an average of 1600 to 1800 pounds of hops can be raised. A few hop lice—so called—were among my hops this last season, but did not do much damage. How it will be in the future it will be hard to tell, but I am not much afraid of them, as it will not cost more than from one to two cents per pound to fight them.

The cost of putting out a hop yard is: For poles, planting hops and setting poles, about $50 per acre, and for a kiln, 24x24, storing room, press and 75 boxes, capable of drying 12 tons, $800.

BRITISH COLUMBIA AS A FRUIT GROWING COUNTRY IN COMPARISON WITH ONTARIO.

PAPER BY G. W. HENRY, PORT HAMMOND.

Mr. President and Gentlemen,

In speaking on British Columbia as a fruit growing country, I have more particularly brought it into comparison with Ontario, for the reason that at the present time all those who have been, and still are, planting out orchards are doing so, to a great extent, with the hope of supplying the fast increasing markets of the North-west and Manitoba with fruit in the near future.

We are situated at about an equal distance from these points as is Ontario, and have about the same facilities for shipping, etc. It is, therefore, a matter of the greatest consequence to us to know what our chances are likely to be for the supply of that trade.

We find that we can only produce very much the same varieties of fruit as can be grown in Ontario; but to know just what varieties can be *most* successfully produced here, and *least* favorably there, is the important question.

I have had a good deal of experience with Ontario fruit, not only in growing it, putting it up, shipping it to various home and foreign markets, but also in handling it in these markets, and since coming to this country, have been considerably engaged in the same way with fruits here. I have therefore had a very good opportunity to gain knowledge on the subject.

I do not mean to intimate that after the supplying of our own markets we can expect to look no farther than to the North-west and Manitoba for a market any more than Ontario does *now;* for as she annually exports many thousands of barrels of apples to England and other countries, so may we, at no very distant date, expect to ship many thousands of packages of various kinds of fruit to different parts of the world each year.

There have been a great many exaggerated statements gone abroad in regard to the fruit growing of this country, and, like all false reports, have done more or less harm. Probably some intending to recommend it have done the most harm. These statements have not been false so much as to what *can* be done here as to what *has* been done. For we all know that fruit generally as it has been grown and put up here certainly has not been such as to recommend British Columbia as a favorable fruit producing country; but through all this the observant horticulturist could see that there are great possibilities, and the fault lies with the grower and not with the country. This state of things is fast changing, and a better class of trees are now being planted, and better varieties of fruit, and we hope soon to see a corresponding improvement in the putting it up and handling.

It is well known that the first fruit, both in importance and general culture, is the apple, for by a judicious selection of varieties, and by care in their preservation, they may be had in their natural condition the greater part of the year. They have, therefore, come to be looked upon in this and many other countries as a household necessity instead of a luxury as other fruits; in fact, they hold the place among fruits which potatoes do among vegetables.

In considering apples we, no doubt, take British Columbia more at a disadvantage in comparing with Ontario than in any other fruit; for although we can produce them of larger size and a more abundant yield, yet, as a rule, we lack the fine autumn weather to give them the color, flavor and keeping qualities obtained in Ontario.

It has been often remarked that the apples are not of so good a flavor in this country as eastern apples. The cause is plain to see why in many cases this is so; but it is not *always* so, for we can grow summer apples of equally as fine flavor and appearance and larger in size, and when we happen to get a favorable autumn, our winter apples are not far behind in any respect.

It may thus be seen that Ontario, with her large bearing orchards, the reputation and great keeping qualities of her winter apples, together with the cheap labor and fine system of handling them, will, for some time at least, have the advantage over this part of the province for the supply of winter apples for the markets of Manitoba and the North-west. But there is a spot in British Columbia (perhaps many of them, but one in particular which I would mention) where winter apples can be produced that will, I believe, surpass even those of Ontario—that is the famed Okanagan Valley, for I believe that there the fruit will be as large and the yield as prolific as here, and the appearance and quality equal to Ontario, with a more certain surety of a good crop each year; but this is only a limited area, and, I believe, it is only in isolated spots through the upper country that this can be done, unless some system of irrigation be entered into, giving more advantages than the present natural supply of water offers.

We had a very good example of the bad effect caused to the appearance and flavor of fruit from continued wet weather last season during the time strawberries were ripening. Although we got size to the berries, we got neither color, flavor, nor keeping qualities, and, to a certain extent, the effect is the same on winter apples and other fruits which come to maturity during the rainy weather, which generally occurs in the latter part of September and October.

In regard to the summer fruits, such as the cherry, plum, prune and early pears, there is no doubt that for early bearing of the trees, size and quality of the fruit and prolificacy of yield, we can far surpass Ontario or almost any country, so that we can reasonably expect, when we have sufficient grown, to almost entirely control the markets of Manitoba and the North-west in these fruits.

In the case of peaches and grapes it may be rather premature for one to express an opinion when they have been so little tried. Yet I think I have seen enough to warrant me in saying there are parts of this district which can produce fine peaches as favorably as any country, and though we may not be able to depend on getting a profitable crop of grapes so near the coast every year, there are favored places where, I believe, they can be grown in sufficient quantities and to such an advantage as to warrant people in planting enough to at least supply our own demands to a great extent.

I need scarcely mention the smaller fruits, such as currants, gooseberries, raspberries, strawberries, etc. The past few years have shown what we can do in that line, and there is no doubt that in a few years a great many tons of these fruits will annually be shipped across the mountains.

My advice, therefore, would be, to those who intend entering into fruit growing as a business, that they should plant more extensively of such fruits as the plum, prune, cherry, pear, and, when favorably situated, peaches, rather than too many apples; but for the ordinary farmer, who does not intend to make a specialty of fruit, he no doubt would do better to stick pretty closely to apples (excepting enough for family use of other fruits), for the reason that apples can be much easier produced, and require less care and attention in growing, and can be marketed as easily as any other farm produce, requiring only to be properly assorted and put up in standard packages in the right manner, with the same care that any good farmer would use in disposing of any of his products.

But the growing of all the summer fruits requires constant care and attention, especially at the time of gathering and marketing, which comes on usually when the farmers are most busy with their other harvest, and the fruit, in their eyes being of least consequence, is naturally neglected and to a great extent wasted.

There is another means of disposing of fruit besides shipping it in its natural condition which has already been gone into to a certain extent in this country, and through which we can, no doubt, in a few years compete favorably with any other part of the world. This is the evaporating and canning process. By means of these systems we can not only dispose of all fruit that cannot well be shipped in its green state to advantage, but, owing to the early returns and abundant yields of our orchards, we can, in time, grow fruit entirely for these purposes to a great advantage, thus opening the markets of the world to us.

In conclusion, I would say, after taking all these facts into consideration, the man who enters into fruit growing in this country in an intelligent manner at the present time, need have no fear or doubt as to the ultimate success of his undertaking, for at no distant date, I am certain, we will not only be able to compete favorably for the markets of our own North-west and Manitoba with the most of our green fruits, but in the various markets of the world with canned and evaporated fruits. So there is every reason to look forward to a brilliant future for the fruit grower of British Columbia.

PEPARING ORCHARDS.

PAPER BY N. BUTCHART, PORT MOODY.

There are two ways in planting an orchard. The square way of planting is planting on a square with each tree at right angles and same distance apart from each other, which is the most common way. The other is called the quincunx plan. Each tree is planted on a triangle. The trees in one row are opposite the spaces in the next row. Each tree is equally distant from six others. In this plan there is a greater space left for the admission of light and the trees may also be planted at a less distance apart from each other than in the square. The latter way of planting will take about fifteen per cent. more trees per acre—that is to say, an acre in the square planting would take about 69 trees, each 25 feet apart, whereas the quincunx planting would take about 80 trees at the same distance apart, and have more light, air and sun. This system would also be an advantage in the heavy clearing of land in British Columbia.

The easiest, quickest and most simple way to mark out a common field orchard is with the use of a surveyor's pocket compass : run your lines around its boundary at right angles until you come to the point you started from, making a variation of exactly 90 degrees at each angle, at the same time getting the measurement of each angle ; then mark off the boundary of your orchard at the regular distance you intend planting your trees by placing a double row of pickets on one side and end of the orchard and a single row on the other side and end ; then commence planting your trees at the farthest corner from the double row of pickets, in which manner you may continue digging holes and planting trees until your orchard is finished, always planting towards the double row of stakes. In this way not many stakes are needed, but if the land is very stumpy more of these will be required. By the above arrangement a large plough can be run backwards and forwards on each row, which will save a great deal of digging where the trees are planted.

HOW TO PLANT A TREE.

PAPER BY W. J. BRANDRITH, NORTH ARM.

It has been said, and no doubt truthfully, that three-fourths of all trees planted never become properly developed specimens, and in consequence are not productive. On the contrary, they are not only a serious loss of time and money, but a serious disappointment to the planter, so discouraging him that he will not plant again, and his neighbors point to his losses and claim that

"Trees don't do well here anyway," the cause of horticulture getting such a setback that several successes fail to overcome it.

The best of trees are spoiled by bad planting. A man must be taught how to plant a tree before he can do it properly. A man who has never been taught will almost certainly dig a hole as if for a post, push the roots in a foot or so below the level of the surface, cover them with manure, stamp it down and, like as not, raise a mound around it, and, of course, never dream of using a knife to either root or top. The way to plant a tree in properly drained soil is to dig the hole large enough to admit all the roots in a natural position, and without crowding. Finely pulverized soil must be worked around the roots with the hands or a dibble, the roots covered to a depth of four inches or so and well firmed, the whole finished by spreading three or four inches of partly rotted manure on the surface and for a foot or more beyond the ends of the roots. If the soil is such that it cannot be easily drained, the land may be plowed in ridges, and in place of digging holes, the roots may be set on the surface or nearly so, and earth to cover them may be taken from around, adding the manure as before advised. Each tree will then be on a mound, and it is important that this be at least four feet wider than the spread of the roots, or in other words, the ends of the roots should be two feet from the outside of the mound. It is surprising how well trees grow and bear when this plan is adopted in wet soils. It is essential, however, that these mounds be thoroughly mulched during the summer to keep the soil moist and thus cause the roots to form near the surface, producing fruit bearing wood.

There are three important points to be kept in mind when planting, viz: First, always make the hole much larger than the spread of the roots ; second, never set the stem deeper than it was in the nursery ; third, never to plant a tree when the soil is very wet.

Although I have told you how to plant a tree, it will avail you nothing if you do not know how to prepare the tree for planting. It is here where experience and good judgment are required.

We will suppose your tree is a three year old from the nursery, in the digging the roots are broken and fully one-half of them left in the ground. The treatment they should receive is a matter of vital importance if we would plant trees to live. As the roots are so will the growth be. As a rule too much attention is paid to the tops, and too little to the roots ; (I mean that people buy trees with large tops and think they are gaining time by doing so.) A tree with a small top and plenty of healthy fibrous roots, in good soil, will arrive at a profitable bearing state long before a tree with a large top and a few roots. Let us look to the roots then. They are the motive power that moves the tree along. If damaged they must be repaired and put in working order when planting.

That you may the better understand this important part of the planting, I have brought these trees that you may see how it is done. Although the roots are broken and jagged, it is not of serious consequence if they are rightly treated. A jagged wound in the flesh heals slowly, a clean cut quickly, so with the roots of trees. If planted in the torn and broken condition, the result is decay, and few fibrous roots issue to support the tree, and little, if any growth appears. (See tree.) Now, if the jagged ends of the roots are smoothly cut, the result will be that the wounds heal quickly, the ends swell and fibres start out freely, pushing the tree into vigorous growth.

We must now turn our attention to the top, for do what we will with the roots, the tree is still out of proportion, and planted thus, the root is not equal to the task of supporting the entire top. As a guide to the proper pruning at this time, a safe rule to follow is to cut out all small shoots and cut back the larger ones intended for the framework of the tree, to within three or four buds of their base. The result of this line of action is to be seen in this tree.

PLANT LICE.

PAPER BY T. WILSON, HARRISON RIVER.

Wherever vegetation abounds we may find one or more species of Aphids drawing its food supplies from the leaves and stems of the plants. The one most common hereabouts is the *green fly*, which, during the past season, was very prevalent on our young apple trees, and in many cases the attacks were so bad as to stop the growth for a time. Those pests fasten their beaks in the tender herbage, and successive generations will live and die without changing places, and were they not killed off by other carnivorous insects which prey upon them, they would soon destroy the plants infested by them. I noticed a species of black ant that did a good deal of execution among them, but when it is known that a single aphis in the course of a season may, through its generations, be the progenitor of six billions of descendants, it is not to be wondered at that the pest spreads. It also appears, in some cases, that the male insect is not required, as the females will found a colony and rear and carry them safely through successive generations without the help of the other sex.

I don't know if scaleybug is general in this country or not, but I have found some young trees in the bush badly infested with it. I have seen it often in the Old Country, and also in India in the jungles—in spots that had no access of currents of fresh air, and which were always close and damp, the stems of the young underwood were always covered. That which I found here was just in such a situation, and I only found stems of one species infested, viz., the large bearberry. To the casual observer it only looked like a greyish roughness on the bark, but when examined closely was found to consist of innumerable little white and brown specks, some of them as large as a pin head and oval in shape. When scraped down with a knife, the blade was stained with bloody like matter and the stem of the tree was left in the same state. I believe some of the orchards in California are very bad with this, and I heard lately that in Chilliwhack this is almost the only pest they have.

CULTIVATION OF THE STRAWBERRY.

BY W. W. HILBERN, HORTICULTURIST, CENTRAL EXPERIMENTAL FARM, OTTAWA

This plant requires a cool, rich soil, moist, but not wet, with room to grow. The weeds must be kept down and protection afforded from sudden changes of temperature, resulting in alternate freezing and thawing during the winter and early spring. If these conditions are secured and suitable varieties planted, success is almost sure to follow.

Any soil that will produce a good crop of potatoes or other vegetables will answer for strawberries. It should be well drained, either naturally or by tile drains. A rich clay loam is preferable and will usually give the largest yield, but the fruit will not ripen as early as on sandy loam. Avoid if possible a stiff, heavy clay. While a clay loam will give the best results if properly managed, it will not prove satisfactory unless well drained and the soil thoroughly prepared in the autumn previous to planting.

PREPARATION OF THE SOIL.

For profitable growing on a large scale, select a piece of well drained clay loam. This should receive a heavy coating of manure in the spring and then be either summer-fallowed or planted with potatoes, vegetables or some other early crop which can be removed in time to permit of a proper preparation of the land in autumn before it becomes too wet with fall rains. A sub-soiler should follow the common plough, one that will stir up the subsoil to the depth of five to ten inches without bringing any of it to the top. Sub-soiling is not absolutely necessary, but land thus loosened up will retain moisture longer in time of drought and dry off much more rapidly after heavy rains. The last ploughing in the fall should be thoroughly done and suitable furrows provided so that all surface water may run off quickly. Early in the spring, as soon as the weather and the condition of the soil will permit, cultivate deeply both lengthwise and crosswise with a two-horse cultivator; harrow down smooth and the land will be ready for planting. Avoid ploughing a heavy soil in the spring for immediate planting.

Gravelly or sandy loam should be heavily manured in the spring, and may be planted with vegetables. All weeds should be kept down during the summer. Plough in the fall and again in the following spring, and harrow thoroughly. No subsequent tillage will make up for inadequate preparation of the soil for strawberry culture. A stiff clay loam is more difficult to manage. A crop of clover or other green manure turned under will help to make the soil more friable. Coarse barnyard manure should also be used whenever it can be applied in time to decompose and become well mixed with the soil before planting. Tile drains in such soil require to be much nearer together and should not be too deep, usually not more than two and a half feet. In the autumn, before the land becomes too wet, trench it up in high, narrow ridges ; if done with the plough, turn two furrows together, forming a sharp ridge as when prepared for carrots or other roots. Surface drains should be made to take off surplus water quickly. When thus exposed to the action of the frost, a comparatively heavy soil will work down fine and mellow in the spring and give good results. Care must be taken, however, never to stir such soil when wet, either with hoe, plough or cultivator.

TIME TO PLANT.

Plant as early in the spring as the land can be prepared, as this gives the whole season for growth, and enables the plants to produce a good crop the following year. Fall planting, if done in August, will yield a small crop the following spring, but seldom enough to pay for the extra labor required. The principal objection to fall planting is that the plants do not make sufficient root growth to prevent them from lifting in the soil with the repeated freezing and thawing to which they are exposed during the winter and early spring. In any locality where no difficulty is likely to occur from this cause, autumn planting may often be practised with advantage.

METHODS OF PLANTING.

Several different systems have been practised successfully. The method of planting should be regulated by the quantity of land to be used, the amount of manure and labor at the disposal of the planter, the varieties to be planted, whether for market, or for a city garden, or on the farm for family use.

HILL SYSTEM.

For a city garden, where land is usually scarce, the hill system will generally give very satisfactory results. Plant in rows two feet apart and twelve to fifteen inches apart in the row. Cut off all runners before they have time to take root, thus enabling the plants to make strong stools or bills by the end of the growing season. Any blossoms which appear the same season of planting should be removed. In an unfavorable locality, where much alternate freezing and thawing is likely to occur during winter and early spring, growing in hills is not always successful, as they are more likely to heave with the frost, and the plants do not afford the same protection to each other as when planted in matted rows.

MATTED ROWS.

For this mode of culture, the rows require to be from two and a half to four feet apart, and the plants twelve to fifteen inches apart in the row. Cut off all blossoms which may appear, also the first runners, until the plants have gained sufficient vigor to send out several strong runners at once, when they should be allowed to take root and form a matted row from six to twelve inches in width. All free growing sorts make too many plants and should have all surplus runners cut off. The plants should not be crowded in the row. From three to six inches apart each way will give the required protection to each other and room to produce fruit of large size and in abundance.

WHAT TO PLANT.

At a meeting of the Fruit Growers' Association a special committee was appointed to gather what information they could and report upon what varieties of fruit they thought were best to grow for profit in British Columbia. After considerable investigation by this committee it was decided to recommend the following varieties :

Apples—Early summer, Yellow Transparents, Red Astrachan ; late summer, Oldenburg, Gravenstein, ; fall, Wealthy, King ; winter, Northern Spy, Baldwin, Golden Russet, Ben Davis, Canada Red. Sweet apples—Summer, Golden Sweet ; fall, Bailey's Sweet ; winter, Talman's Sweet.

Crabs—Transcendent, Hyslop, Montreal Beauty.

Pears—Summer, Clapp's Favorite, Bartlett, ; fall, Beurre, Clairgeau, Beurre d'Anjou ; winter, Lawrence, Beurre Easter.

Plums—Peach plums, Bradshaw, Imperial Gage, Lombard, Red Egg, Yellow Egg, Reine Claude de Bavay.

Prunes—Italian, Pond's Seedling, Coes' Golden Drop.

Cherries—Sweet, Early Purple Guigne, Governor Wood, Black Tartarian, Napoleon Bigarreau (Royal Ann), Yellow Spanish, Windsor. Cherries—sour, May Duke, Large Montmorenci, English Morello.

Peaches—Alexander, Waterloo, Early Rivers, Hale's Early, Early Crawford and Wager.

Apricots and Nectarines—Not sufficiently tested to be recommended.

Quince—Orange.

Grapes—Moore's Early, black ; Worden, black ; Delaware, red ; Brighton, red ; Niagara, white ; Concord, black.

Strawberries—Crescent, Wilson, Sharpless, Bubach No. 5, Improved Jocunda.

Raspberries—Marlborough, Cuthbert, Golden Queen.

Black caps—Louhegan, Tyler, Gregg.

Blackberries—Snider, Kittatiny, Erie, Taylor.

English gooseberries—Industry, liable to mildew in some localities.

American—Champion, Downing.

Red currants--Fay's Prolific, Moore's Ruby, Cherry currant.

White—White Grape.

Black—Lee's Prolific, Black Champion, Black Naples.

List of Varieties not thoroughly tested but worthy of trial—Apples, summer, Keswick, Codlin, Alexander; fall, Haas, Colvert, Princess Louise, Maiden's Blush, Red Betigheimer; winter, Pewaukee, McIntosh's Red, Hubbardson's Nonesuch, Seek-no-further, Rhode Island Greening, Grimes' Golden, Stark, Newtown Pippin, Yellow Bellflower.

Pears—Summer, Madeline, Marguerite, Brockworth Park; fall, Beurre Bossock, Duchess d'Angouleine, Howell, Sheldon; winter, Josephine de Malines.

Plums—Genii, McLaughlan, Moore's Arctic, Jefferson, Shipper's Pride, Smith's Orleans.

Cherries—Rockport Bigarreau, Olivet, Mezel, Black Republican.

Peaches--Foster, Shumaker, Wheatland and Coolidges Favorite.

Grapes—Moore's Diamond; Meyer.

Strawberries--Haverland, Warfield No. 2, Triomphe de Gand.

Apricots--Moorpark, Early Golden, St. Catherine, St. Ambrose, Early Montgamet.

Nectarines—Boston, Early Violet.

Quince--Rhea's Mammoth, Champion.

--- --- ---

ADVICE TO GROWERS AND SHIPPERS OF FRUIT.

The fruit industry of British Columbia is a growing one; in fact, it is practically in its infancy yet, and all growers ought to increase their acreage and encourage new horticulturists to set out orchards, with the firm belief that the fruit business is *not* overdone nor likely to be overdone in the near (or even remote) future.

Our markets for all varieties of fruit are increasing in number, and the territory into which fruit has been shipped during the season of 1891 extends eastward to the Atlantic.

The demand is continually increasing for all the better varieties of apples, pears, plums, prunes, peaches, and cherries, and we would suggest to those contemplating the setting out of new orchards or the increasing of their former acreage, to consult the commercial demands as well as the suitability of location. The serious mistake in the past has been the number of varieties of trees planted as compared with the total number of trees. Avoid this error. If you have ground cleared for five hundred trees, it is better, for your own interest, to plant the entire amount in one class of fruit, even though you select two or three varieties from that class. In many instances it would even be best to have the entire lot of one variety. Orchardists should understand that they are not raising their fruit for home consumption; their largest profits will be in the shipping trade. And if they have a sufficient quantity of any one variety of fruit to load a car, they are in a position to dictate prices to the shipper, whereas if they have but a small portion of a car, and the shipper is compelled to look into a dozen orchards in order to buy a sufficient quantity of one given variety to make up a car load, the shipper can dictate. Another view is this: wherever large orchards exist, there the larger buyers congregate first, and the owner of the orchard realizes all the benefits of active competition among the buyers. California horticulturists know this, and are making money by having large orchards and plenty of each variety of fruit.

Those owning old orchards should take every means to clean them and keep them so Cut out all the old branches and trim up the tree generally. *Burn your rubbish.* Don't let it remain piled up in a corner near a fence, for such piles are the breeding grounds of all kinds of pests. Burn it at once. Don't let the weeds grow in your orchard, but keep the ground thoroughly cultivated all the time. It will pay you well in the long run.

MARKETING FRUIT.

It is hard to explain just how ripe fruit should be when picked for market. In all instances, it is best to consult the wishes of the shipper or dealer. If fruit is intended for the local market, it should be ripe enough for immediate use, and yet firm enough to "stand up" for two or three days before showing signs of decay. For shipping purposes, much depends on the distance the fruit is to go and the length of time it is expected to "stand up" before reaching the consumer. Take the suggestion of the shipper in every instance, for, as a rule, he knows what he wants and how he wants it. The writer, during the past season, has had much success with shipping peach-plums, simply because they were picked before they had their full growth and just after they had turned from green to their peculiar white cast—before getting even a blush of color. During previous seasons he has lost money on them because he has invariably waited for them to get a "blush" before picking them for distant shipping purposes.

PEACHES.

Peaches, for distant shipment, should be firm and fairly well colored, and wrapped and packed in boxes containing about 20 pounds net of fruit. Grade the fruit so as to make two tier boxes of the larger and three tier boxes of the smaller peaches. Don't ship anything under a three tier peach to market; it is not saleable, and being offered, hurts the sale of the better stock. For local use, riper peaches should be packed in common splint baskets containing about 18 pounds.

PEARS.

All varieties of pears should be picked as soon as they will leave the trees without pulling or breaking the stem. A gentle twist of the wrist should bring the fruit off the tree. Don't bruise the fruit in transferring it from your baskets to the orchard boxes, and under no circumstances gather fallen fruit for shipment. For distant shipment, pears should be wrapped and packed in standard pear boxes containing 45 pounds of fruit.

APPLES.

All varieties should be carefully gathered in their season and allowed to remain in orchard boxes or small heaps for a week or more before packing for shipment. Cull out all small or wormy fruit, and be sure you pack only selected apples. It does not pay to send unmerchantable apples or any unsaleable fruit to market. Always use new standard boxes and face the first layer. Then fill in the box tightly and full, so that when the bottom is nailed down not an apple in the box will move in its place. Make your name, branded on the box, a guarantee of the quality of the fruit contained therein, and you will soon see how shippers will seek your brand and pay top prices to secure you pack. It pays big to build up such a reputation.

DRIED FRUIT.

Every large orchardist should have an evaporator of some kind on his place. All over-ripe fruit, and fruit that is too inferior for the market, can be easily taken care of in a small evaporator. If you have a large prune orchard, a good sized evaporator will be necessary. Of the different systems of drying, it will be impossible to say anything in this article. Each system has its peculiarities, its advantages and disadvantages. Use only new boxes (either 25 or 50 pound standard spruce boxes) or new cotton sacks for marketing your dried fruit. When packing in boxes, line them first with clean white paper and next to that lay a sheet of waxed paper. Always face your fruit on this sheet of waxed paper, then fill in to the required weight and press into the box. The neater the package and the style of packing, the more readily your dried fruit will sell, and the higher the price realized therefor.

Attractiveness has much to do with the selling qualities of everything offered. Your fruit may be equal, and perhaps superior, to that of your neighbor's, but if your neighbor has packed his fruit more carefully or more attractively, he has undoubtedly been able to sell his output for a higher price than you.

PEST ✣ REMEDY

SUPPLEMENT

As adopted by a Committe

APPOINTED AT THE

ANNUAL MEETING

OF THE

HORTICULTURAL SOCIETY

AND

FRUIT GROWERS' ASSOCIATION

OF

BRITISH COLUMBIA

JANUARY, 1892.

FOR MUCH OF THE INFORMATION GIVEN WE ARE INDEBTED
TO THE EXCELLENT BULLETINS OF THE STATE BOARDS
OF HORTICULTURE OF OREGON AND WASHINGTON ALSO
TO THE BULLETINS OF THE EXPERIMENTAL FARM
OTTAWA.

Pests and Remedies.

USEFUL INFORMATION FOR FRUIT GROWERS
GATHERED FROM RELIABLE
SOURCES.

Most seasons, from November to April, is the time for thorough work in destroying fruit pests in orchards, on various trees and plants of this province.

It is the only season when successful work is done with a view to exterminate the pests, entirely without injury to plant life.

Summer spraying is beneficial, but results only in holding the damaging insects in check, while the washes given in this supplement for winter spraying are of such strength as will destroy the egg germs if properly applied. The soap and lye, also the sulphur and lime washes are excellent fertilizers, and will benefit trees wherever applied. These washes should be used in every orchard.

Every person purchasing young trees should see that the same have been disinfected, as advised in this supplement.

The San Jose Scale or Greedy Scale and Woolly Aphis are the insects to be guarded against more than any other, and for protection it will pay to wash every tree being planted, or that is now in the orchard.

Merchants should be forbidden to dispose of fruit boxes, etc., for the use of fruit again, unless fumigated. All growers should avoid the practice of picking up boxes promiscuously from fruit stands, unless they have been thoroughly disinfected, because from this source many orchards have been infested.

There are many beneficial insects, which destroy the injurious insects; the practice of "growers" should be to learn to distinguish these and their habits, in order to best protect them. Most birds are of great benefit to horticulturists, in destroying the injurious insects, and should be protected.

THE CODLIN MOTH.

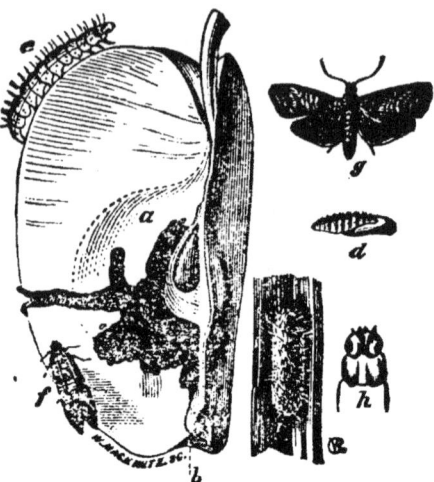

The puncture made by the moth is represented at (b), the borings of the larva at (a), the mature worm at (e), the moth with wings closed at (f), the moth with wings expanded at (g), and the cocoon at (i); (d), the chrysalis, and (h), the anterior part of the body, magnified.

This insect, which appears in the early worm-eaten apples and pears, in the form of a reddish white grub, was introduced into this country with the apple tree from Europe. It causes the fruit to fall prematurely from the trees. "The perfect insect," says Charles Downing, in his work on *Fruit and Fruit Trees of America*, "is a small moth; the fore wings grey with large round brown spots on the hinder margin. These moths appear in the greatest number in the warm evenings of June, and lay their egg in the eye or blossom end of the young fruit, especially of the early kinds of apples and pears. In a short time, these eggs hatch and the grub burrows its way till it reaches the core. The fruit then ripens immediately and drops to the ground, here the worm leaves the fruit and creeps into the crevices of the bark and hollow of the tree and spins its cocoon, which usually remains there till ensuing spring when the young moth again emerges from it.

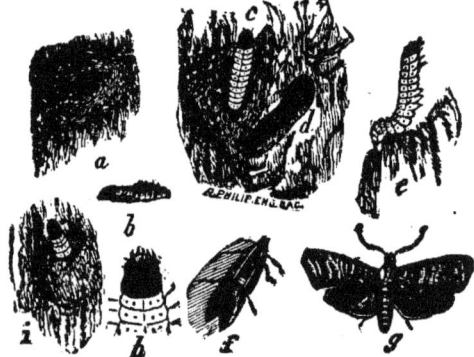

(a) Nest of larva on outside of tree, under the old bark; (b) pupa; (c) larva exposed from nest; (d) old nest; (e) larva about to build nest; (f) the moth at rest; (g) moth with wings spread; (h) head of larva.

REMEDIES AGAINST THE CODLIN MOTH.

There are two modes of fighting them generally made use of—one is to prevent the hatching of the egg, or the killing of the young worm while working into the fruit ; the other is the catching of the worm in traps as it is escaping from the fruit, or having the fruit eaten by hogs as soon as it drops from the tree and before the worm escapes. The first mode is without doubt · the most successful, and is also the least expensive. This is accomplished by spraying the trees with London purple or Paris green, using one pound of either to one hundred and fifty gallons of water. Paris green is a compound of arsenic and copper. It is a far more powerful poison than arsenic alone, and is not soluble in water, hence it will remain much longer on the trees. London purple is another arsenical compound. It is the residue from the manufacture of aniline dye, and contains lime, arsenuous acid and carbonaceous matter. It is soluble, more adhesive and less poisonous than Paris green. It is better to wet the powder thoroughly and make a paste before putting it into the vessel of water, that it may not form lumps. The liquid should then be strained, thereby removing the sediment that is in the London purple. Some have reported to this Board, that the London purple burned the foliage. This, doubtless, arises from difference in the strength of the London purple, and we recommend that care be exercised and tests be made before using, so that it shall not be too strong. The spray is caused by forcing the liquid, by means of a force pump, through a fine perforated nozzle, made specially for the purpose. The finer it is the less liquid will be required. The important thing is to scatter the spray on all the fruit.

• WHEN TO SPRAY.

The Codlin Moth, soon after the fruit sets, lays her eggs upon the calyx or blossom end of the young fruit. The grub, as soon as hatched, eats its way into the centre of the sound fruit, and there, growing with its growth, works its mischief. In its early state the young fruit is erect, its calyx or blossom end upwards, and the least particle of poisoned water falling upon it is sufficient to destroy the young worm when it attempts to eat its way into the fruit. Therefore, the best and most opportune time for spraying the tree is soon after the fruit is set, and when it is about the size of a small pea. Experience teaches, however, that it is not safe to depend upon the one early spraying to accomplish the results sought for, whether coming from a second, and perhaps a third, crop, which many affirm and others deny, or from those that from some cause have not matured as rapidly as others ; still the facts remain that in many places the Codlin Moth does not sting the fruit and lay the eggs until later in the season. Therefore, to obtain the best results, the spraying should be continued with an interval of two weeks until the first of August, and even later than this on some varieties. Care should be observed that vegetables are not sprayed with these mixtures, and no animals be allowed to eat the grass that has been saturated with the spray, and that the spraying is not done when the trees are in bloom, for then it is that bees are present.

THE APPLE TREE APHIS.

During the winter there may be found in the crevices and crooks of the bark of the twigs of the apple tree, and also about the base of the buds, a number of very minute oval, shining black eggs ; these are the eggs of the Apple Tree Aphis, also called the green Aphis, and Apple Tree Louse. These eggs are deposited in the autumn, and when first laid are of a light yellow or green color, but gradually become darker and finally black. As soon as the buds begin to expand in the spring, these eggs hatch very tiny lice, which locate themselves upon the swelling buds and the small tender leaves, and inserting their beaks feed upon the juices. All of the lice then hatched are females, and reach maturity in ten or twelve days, when they commence to give birth to living young, producing about two daily for two or three weeks, after which the older ones die. The young locate about the parents as closely as they can stow themselves, and they also mature and become mothers in ten or twelve days, and are as prolific as their predecessors ; they thus increase so rapidly, that as fast as new leaves expand, colonies are ready to occupy them. As the season advances, some of the lice acquire wings, and dispersing found new colonies on other trees. When cold weather approaches, males as well as females are produced, and the season closes with the deposit of a stock of eggs for the continuance of the species another year. The leaves of trees infested by these insects become distorted and twisted backwards, often with their tips pressing against the twig from which they grow, and they thus form a covering for the Aphis, protecting them from rain. An infested tree may be distinguished at some distance by this bending back of the leaves and young twigs. It is stated that the scab on the apple often owes its origin to the punctures of these plant lice.

REMEDIES.

Very much can be accomplished in the destruction of the eggs that have been deposited upon the bark and in the crevices of the trees during the winter months while the trees are in a dormant condition, by scraping the dead bark off of the trees, and washing or spraying them with a solution of lye water, made by dissolving one pound of Gillet's concentrated lye in five gallons of water, care being observed not to use this strength of wash after the buds have commenced to swell ; this strength of wash will also remove the moss from the limbs and bark of the tree, as well as destroying the larvæ of the Codlin moth which may be reached by it. A frost occurring after a few days of warm weather will kill millions of them. In the egg state, the insect can endure any amount of frost, but the young Aphis quickly perishes when the temperature falls below the freezing point.

The Lady Bird or Lady Bug is one of the most beneficial of the insect tribes to the horticulturalist, from the fact that they prey on other insects in all stages of their growth, from the larvæ to the perfect beetle. These should be propogated and protected so far as possible in orchards afflicted with the Aphis, for myriads of them are devoured by the Lady Bird and their larvæ.

There are a number of solutions that will operate successfully in exterminating the Aphis, and can be used as most convenient to be procured. The merit of these solutions is considered in the order named:

SOLUTION NO. 4.—SAL SODA AND LYE.

SOLUTION NO. 5.—WHALE OIL SOAP AND KEROSENE.

SOLUTION NO. 6.—TOBACCO AND SOAP.

(a).—"Take air slacked lime and dust on tree; is more effectual when tree is damp with dew or otherwise."

(b).—"One ounce borax; one ounce whale oil soap in one gallon of water. Dissolve in hot water; apply cold.

(c).—One pound of common laundry soap; one pound washing soda dissolved in sixteen gallons of hot water."

Apply any of these mixtures by means of a spray pump as soon as the eggs begin to hatch, and continue the treatment as long as there is one Aphis to be found.

WOOLLY APHIS.

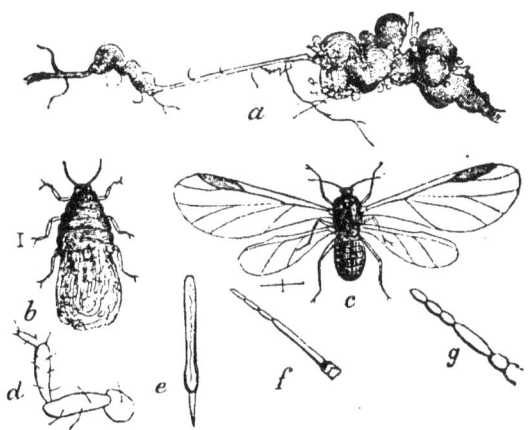

WOOLLY APHIS *(Schizoneura lanigera).* *(*After *Riley).*
(a), an infested root, (b), the larvæ—color, brown; (c), winged adult—colors, black and yellow; (d), its leg; (e), its beak; (f), its antennæ; (g), antennæ of the larva (b); all highly magnified.

This insect is of a dark russet brown color, with the abdomen covered with a white down of a cottony appearance. It attacks the roots, trunks and branches of apple, pear and cherry trees. It does not affect the leaves or fruit.—*Cooke.*

This is, without question, one of the most dangerous enemies to which the apple tree is subjected. That it has secured a strong hold in the larger portion of the orchards in Western Oregon and Washington, and is putting in an appearance east of the Cascades, is to be regretted. So far we can learn but little, if any, effort has been made to exterminate it from any of the orchards infested. This, we think, is due to the fact that but few know what it is, and the danger that its presence brings to the orchard.

The Woolly Aphis is a small insect covered with a white, woolly substance, hence its name. Its color is a reddish brown, and when crushed it yields a red juice. They infest the apple trees in particular, both roots and branches. They live upon the sap of the bark and produce small warts or granulations on it. They increase with astonishing rapidity, and the wind carries them from one tree to another by the light down in which they are enwrapped, and thus they spread quickly from one orchard to another. Not a moment should be lost in destroying the first one that puts in an appearance.

REMEDY.

The following remedy is taken from the secretary's report, California State Board of Horticulture :

"Four pounds of rosin, three pounds of sal soda, water to make four and one-half gallons; dissolve the sal soda in a few pints of water; when thoroughly dissolved add the rosin; heat until dissolved and add water finally. Use one and one-half pints of this solution to the gallon of water. Use at a temperature of 100 degrees Fahrenheit."

The application of any of the remedies used for the destruction of the Green Aphis are also recommended as being good. It is thought by this committee that owing to the dampness of our climate the Woolly Aphis will not infest the roots to any great extent, and that a shovelful or so of fresh ashes placed around the base of the tree will destroy those that may have commenced operations below the surface and prevent others from doing so. In the drier climates of the Interior and east of the mountains, it doubtless will be found that they will do their most destructive work out of sight at the roots. When this is known to be the case, the application of fresh gas lime has proved to be a lasting destroyer of the insect, and also a valuable fertilizer for the tree—a couple of shovelfuls for each tree, spreading it over the surface around the tree to cover about six feet in diameter. If the soil is deep and well drained, a much larger quantity may be safely used. Care should be taken not to put it around the body of the tree, as the solution of gas water formed by the rains might scald the bark. It will be well also to use in connection with the gas lime a shovelful of fresh ashes around the base of the tree. This will prevent possible migration of the Aphis from the roots to the upper branches.

THE APPLE-ROOT PLANT LOUSE.

This insect appears in two forms, one of which attacks the trunks of the apple tree, the other works under the ground and produces on the roots wart-like swellings and excrescences of all shapes and sizes. While it usually confines itself to the roots of trees, it is sometimes found on the suckers that spring up from the roots, and occasionally the mature lice crawl up the branches of the trees, where they also form colonies during summer, and then are known as the Woolly Aphis of the apple. The insect which attacks the trunk and limbs of the apple tree is of the same species as that which works on the root, having the same cotton-like covering. In October a considerable number of these appear with wings, having but little downy substance upon their bodies. Late in the autumn, the females deposit eggs for another generation the following spring, and thus furnish the parents of countless hosts to infest the trees another season.

There are several friendly insects which prey upon this Woolly Aphis. A very minute four-winged fly, *Alphelinus Mali*, is parasitic on it, and the larvæ of a small beetle belonging to the Lady Bird family, *Scymnus Cervacalis*, feeds on it.

SOLUTION NO. 2.—KEROSENE.

During the summer months those on the trees can easily be killed by touching them with a swab dipped in coal oil.

SOAP—FOR YOUNG TREES.

Two pounds of home-made soft soap to one and one-half gallons of water, poured around the roots of the nursery stock (young apple trees), destroy the Woolly Aphis, the earth being first cleared away from the trees. The roots of young apple trees should be dipped before planting.

APPLE TREE BORER.
(Chrysobothris femorata).

(a) Shows larva; (b) chrysalis; (c) primary stage; (d) the perfect insect.

Of these there are a number of species. The two striped or round-headed is extremely destructive to apple orchards, from the boring of the grub into the wood of the trees. The mature beetle appears during May and June, and being strictly nocturnal, is seldom seen except by those who hunt for it. The female deposits her eggs mostly in June, in the bark near the foot of the tree, and also in the forks of the main branches. The eggs hatched, the minute grubs commence boring into the wood, generally downward the first year, and upward and near the bark the second year. The Borer lives in the wood of the tree until the third year, when it emerges as a perfect beetle. It infests healthy as well as unhealthy trees, and is very destructive.

The flat-headed Borers, while working in the same class of trees, is totally unlike the others. Boring an oval hole twice as wide as high, the beetle flies by day instead of at night, and besides the apple tree, attacks the oak, peach, soft maple, ash, willow, tulip, and even the elm and cotton wood; it also attains its full size in one year from the egg. This Borer attacks limbs and trunk indiscriminately.

REMEDY.

The natural enemies of these insects are the birds of the Woodpecker tribe.

Artificial remedies are to find the cast of the larvæ, and kill them by piercing with a flexible wire. Prevention is, however, the only sure remedy. Keep the base of every tree clear of weeds and trash, and apply a solution of soft soap reduced to the consistence of a thick paint by the addition of a strong solution of washing soda in water. This, if applied to the bark of the tree, especially about the base or collar, and thence up the trunk and over the larger branches, will dry in a few hours, and form a tenacious coating not easily dissolved by rain. This soap solution should be applied in May, and a second time the latter part of June.

THE APPLE-TREE TENT CATERPILLAR.

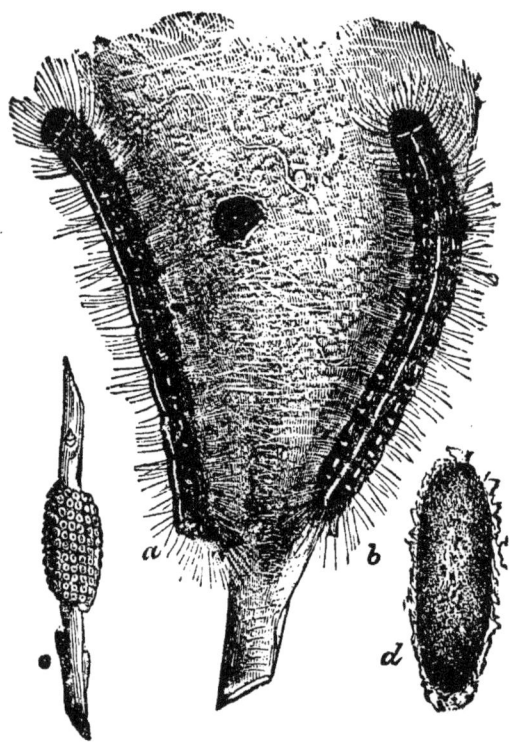

(a) Side view; (b) back view, full grown at about six weeks old; (c) cluster of e (d) cocoon, oval, of pale yellow color.

The moth is of a pale, dull reddish or reddish-brown color, crossed by two oblique parallel whitish lines, being usually paler than the general color, although sometimes quite as dark, or darker. It lives but a few days in the winged state, merely long enough to provide for a future generation, by the deposition of eggs. The moths are usually most abundant during the first two weeks in July. The eggs, conical, and about one-twentieth of an inch long, are deposited in July upon the smaller twigs in ring-like clusters.

The young caterpillars are fully matured in the egg before winter and thus remain until favorable spring weather, when they begin to move about and soon construct for themselves a shelter by extending shoots of web across the nearest fork of the twig upon which they were hatched, for retreat at night and stormy weather. In five or six weeks they become from one inch to one and three quarter inches in length.

REMEDY.

These egg clusters must be sought for during winter months, when the trees being leafless, the eye will readily detect them, after being hatched out, their nests are so conspicuous that there can be no excuse for neglecting to destroy them, and where any of these pests appeared last season thorough search must be made for these rings of eggs (which are generally found on the small branches), collecting and destroying by pouring boiling water on them or by burning them.

Solutions No. 2 and 3, if properly applied will destroy the young larvæ.

THE FOREST TENT CATERPILLAR.

This insect closely resembles the common tent caterpillar described on another page. The eggs are of almost uniform diameter, and from three to four hundred in each cluster, squarely cut off, as shown in (a). After the

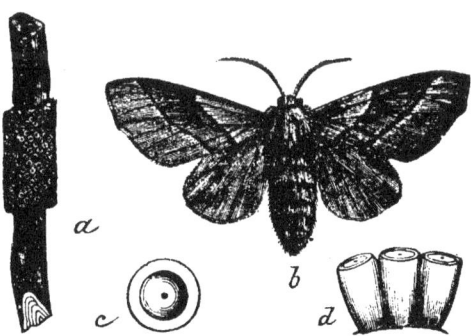

(a), egg cluster : (b), moth ; (c), one of the eggs much enlarged, as seen from the top ; (d), a side view from the same.

insects are hatched in spring they are often seen marching about in single or double column. In about six weeks these insects are full grown, thus :

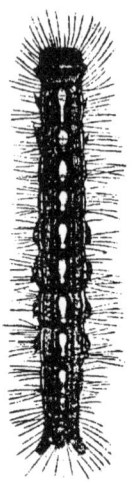

They are from one to one and one-half inches long, pale, bluish color, with black points and dots. On the back is a row of ten or eleven oval or diamond-shaped white spots, by which it may be at once distinguished from the common tent caterpillar, while on the sides there are pale yellowish stripes somewhat broken and mixed with grey. These insects were numerous in several sections last season. In some of the old orchards the foilage of the apple trees was entirely devoured.

While particularly injurious to the apple, the insect also attacks various species of forest trees, such as oak, thorn, ash, basswood, plum, cherry, walnut, etc.

When full grown this larva spins its cocoon in some suitable place, when after two or three days there is a change to a chrysalis of a reddish-brown color, densely clothed with short hair and after two or three weeks the moth appears, when, having deposited its egg, it perishes.

REMEDIES.

These egg clusters must be sought for and destroyed during the winter months. They can be readily detected, and are easily dislodged and destroyed. If left unmolested, they will hatch out in spring and be the cause of much damage. See also, remedy recommended for Apple-Tree Tent Caterpillar.

PLUM CURCULIO.

(Conotrachelus nenuphar. —Herbst).

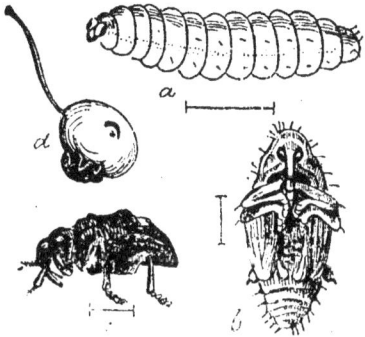

The different stages are shewn in the accompanying wood-cut : (a) represents the grub much magnified ; (b) the chrysalis, and (c) the beetle, both magnified ; (d) the young fruit, shewing the crescent-shaped mark made by the insect, and the curculio, life size, at its work.

There is perhaps no insect so well known by name as the Plum Curculio. The perfect insect belongs to the family known as the snout-beetles, from the shape of the head, which is elongated into a beak. It is a small, rough, grayish beetle, about one-fifth of an inch long. The females lay their eggs in the young fruit of plums and cherries, frequently destroying the whole crops.

REMEDIES.

The beetles are sluggish in the early morning, and drop from the trees if a sudden jar be given to the trunk. For this purpose a metal spike is driven into the trunk, which is struck sharply with an iron hammer. This gives the sharp jar necessary to dislodge the beetles which fall on sheets or into receptacles placed beneath the trees. They are then collected and destroyed.

Of late years abundant evidence has proved the efficacy of spraying the trees, as soon as the fruit has formed, with Paris green, 1 pound, to 200 gallons of water, and ten days afterwards a second time with a weaker mixture, one pound, to 300 gallons. Should heavy rains occur immediately after these sprayings, they must be repeated.

POISONING.

Poisoning by using arsenical poison, Paris green or London purple, the last seems preferable, as it is cheaper, more readily mixed and more effective. One pound to 200 gallons of water is strong enough, spraying trees, Weir says : "First, just before the blossom buds open ; second, two weeks after the petals fall. If a weak, soapy kerosene emulsion is used at this spraying to mix the poisons in, it will also destroy the leaf lice, aphides, bugs and all other insects injurious to the fruit and foliage ; and then a third spraying about June 10th, and your fruit is safe."

PLANTING WILD PLUMS.

These plums planted *en masse* in a sufficient quantity on a place will gather unto themselves all the Plum Curculios on the place, and so protect all other fruit from its ravages. And being on them the female naturally lays her eggs in the fruit, few of which ever hatch, and so few reach maturity in this fruit. The extensive planting of the same on a place will well nigh extermi- nate the pest. — *Weir.*

SAN JOSE SCALE OR GREEDY SCALE.

(*Aspidiotus Perniciosus or Aspidiotus rapax.*)

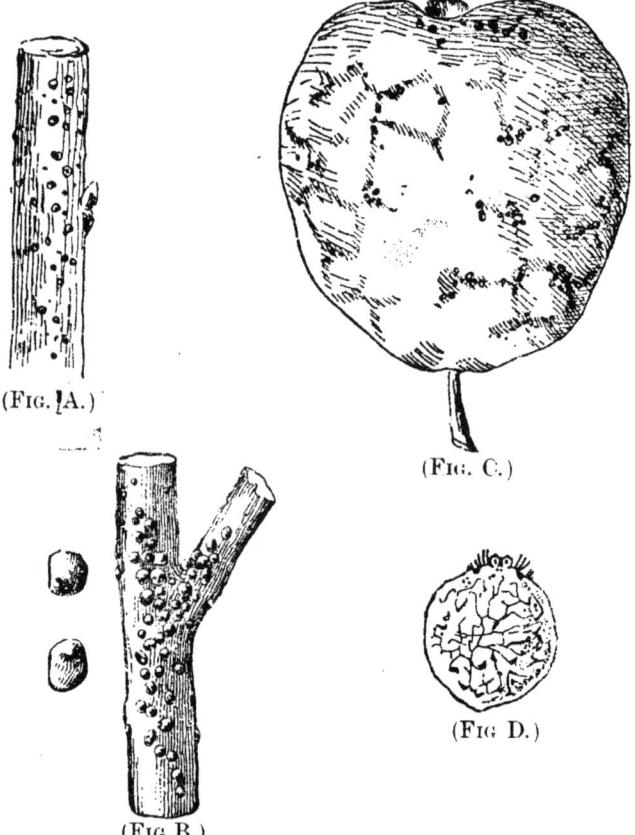

(Fig. A.)

(Fig. C.)

(Fig B.)

(Fig D.)

A and B, portions of branches infested; C, a pear infested; D, larva of female enlarged.

This dreaded and most destructive enemy of not only the fruit, but the ornamental and forest trees as well, has secured a hold in some of the orchards in Oregon and Washington, and it is feared that it will be ultimately found in this province. Careful inquiry from parties with whom the Scale is found, develops the fact that they have been brought into Oregon on trees shipped from California. As trees from California have been pretty generally distribu- ted all over the coast by the industrious tree pedlar, so it may be expected that these destructive insects have doubtless gone with them.

The remedy to be applied to the Scale is much more simple than the one to be applied to the tree pedlar or the careless person who buys his trees without first knowing whether they are coming from infested nurseries or not. The following remedies for the Scale are recommended :

This is, without exception, the most pernicious Scale insect known in this country. It affects all the deciduous trees. They have also been found on some of the evergreen varieties. They infest the bark of the trunk and limbs of the tree, also the leaves and fruit. Their presence upon the bark will soon turn the sap part of the wood beneath the bark to a reddish color. Their presence upon the fruit causes it to be covered with bright red spots, and, when badly affected, the fruit shrivels up and cracks open.

The Scale of the female is circular and flat, gray in color, except the centre, which is of a reddish yellow. The Scale of the male is black, and is somewhat elongated when fully grown. The full grown Scale is scarcely one-sixteenth of an inch in diameter. The eggs are yellow. The young larvæ are very active and of a pale yellow color, and barely to be seen with the naked eye. The young Scales appear like fly-specs. They multiply with great rapidity, there being three broods in one season. The first hatching is usually the latter part of May, the second in July and the third in September.

The fact that they multiply thus rapidly and infest to the death nearly every variety of tree and shrub, makes their presence in our midst one of great danger to not only our fruit trees, but to the shade and ornamental trees as well.

REMEDIES.

This pest is so readily detected during the month of May, that wherever trees are infested they will be noticed at once, and where they were not destroyed last season, the trees or bushes should be sprayed or thoroughly washed during winter with solution No. 2, No. 3 or No. 7.

Solution No. 1.—D. M. Jessee, state pest inspector, says he has tried this solution to his entire satisfaction, and is assured it will destroy these insects more effectually than any other remedy he has used. Notice what is stated as to the strength of solutions, as to summer and winter spraying.

BLACK SPOT OR FUNGUS. (*Fusicladum dendriticum.*)

This disease that the apple and pear are subject to is doing a good deal of damage to those fruits in some portions of British Columbia. It is more apparent and destructive on some varieties than upon others. The causes which produce this disease are somewhat uncertain. Suffice it that those longest in cultivation, most productive, and in confined situations, appear to be most liable to it. It is a fungus growth, presenting, when examined by the microscope, a mossy, spongy character, occupying the skin so as to prevent the development of its tissues, and result in checking the growth at that point, thus creating a black spot and a deformity. When the malady spreads, as it sometimes does, over half or more of the apple or pear, it tends to a deeper nature and causes the fruit to crack open and become corky and worthless. The Department of Agriculture at Washington recommend the use of the following wash to destroy this fungii, to be applied with a spray pump. Care should be observed in following the directions, otherwise the foliage of the tree will be injured by burning.

REMEDY.

Dissolve one pound of sulphate of copper (blue vitrol) in one gallon of hot water. To this solution add liquid ammonia, a little at a time, until all the copper is precipitated. The liquid is then turbid and blue in color. Add two or three gallons of water and let it stand and settle. Then pour off the clear liquid, which contains sulphate of ammonia—the compound which causes the burning of the leaves—then pour upon the precipitate left in the vessel just enough liquid ammonia to dissolve it; the result is a clear liquid of a deep blue color. When required for use, dilute to twenty-two gallons.

PEAR AND CHERRY TREE SLUG.

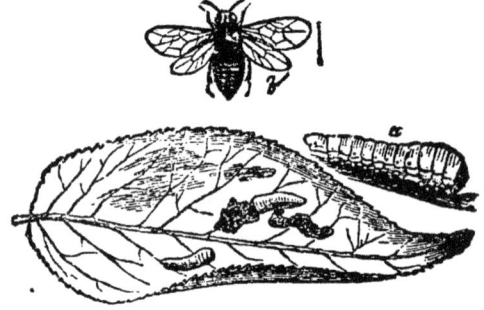

Growers should be on the look-out for this destructive pest about middle of June and again early in August, and if the young slugs are then abundant, they should be then promptly attended to, since if neglected, they soon play sad havoc with the foliage, feeding upon the upper side of the leaves and consuming the tissues, leaving only the veins and under skin. The foliage deprived of its substance, withers and becomes dark colored, as if scorched by fire, and soon afterwards it drops from the tree. Trees badly infested often become as bare of foliage in July as they are in January. In such cases the tree is obliged to throw out new leaves, and this extra effort so exhausts its vigor as to interfere seriously with its fruit producing powers the following year. Although very abundant one season, they may be very scarce the next, as they are liable to be destroyed in the interval by enemies and by unfavorable climatic influences.

REMEDIES.

Spray with Solution No. 1.

The Oregon *Bulletin* recommends the following remedy : London purple or Paris green mixed with water in the proportion of one ounce to six gallons,.

and apply to the foliage with a syringe or a spray pump, as promptly destroying this slug.

Fresh air slacked lime, sand, ashes or road dust on the foliage is said to be an efficient remedy. But these latter are unsatisfactory measures and usually of little value, especially if applied late in the season.

THE OYSTER SHELL BARK LOUSE.

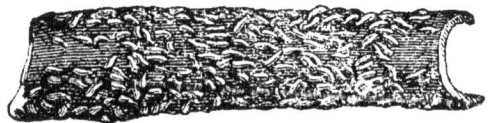

The scale is of a brownish or grayish color, about one-sixth of an inch in length, nearly the color of the bark of the tree, and in shape resembles the shell of an oyster—hence its name.

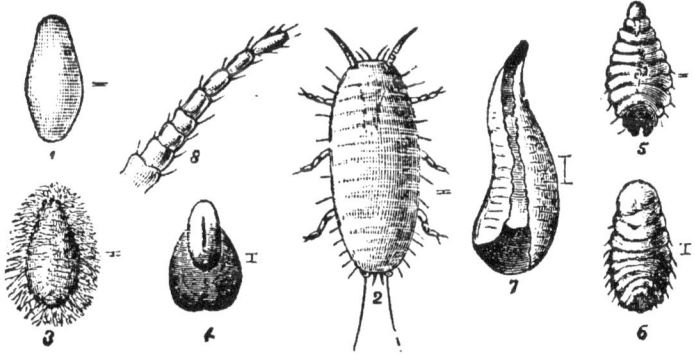

In some instances the branches and trunks of the trees become literally covered with these scales. Under each scale, as shown in the figure above at 1, may be found a mass of from twenty to one hundred eggs. In May or early June and September they hatch, and appear as shown, highly magnified, at 2. In a few days a fringe of delicate, waxy threads issues from their bodies, as seen at 3. Gradually the insect assumes the form shown at 4; 5 and 6 present the larva as nearly full grown and when detached from the scale. Before the end of the season the louse has secreted for itself the scale covering shown at 7, in which it lives and matures.

REMEDIES.

Spray with solution No. 1, heretofore described, at intervals of ten to fifteen days from the 10th of May to June 10th, the same solution for winter wash will prove effectual. The rosin and lye wash (solution No. 7) wilf be found effective, also strong solutions of soap or tobacco.

THE WOOLLY MAPLE BARK LOUSE.

(Pulvinaria innumerabilis.)

The presence of the Woolly Maple Bark Louse is manifested in the spring and early summer by the occurrence upon the twigs of maple trees, especially on the under side, of a brown, circular, leathery scale, about one-quarter of an inch in diameter beneath which is a peculiar fluffy cotton mass, presenting the appearance of Fig. A. In the spring there may be found in each of these masses great numbers (700 to 1000) of small white, spherical eggs.

Early in summer these eggs hatch into young lice, which scatter over the trees wandering about on the twigs and leaves for a few days and finally fixing themselves upon the lower leaf surface insert their beaks and suck out the sap.

This scale infests the maple trees, currant bushes, and fruit trees.

(Fig. A.)

They also attack the quince tree and currant bush.

In autumn the males issue as winged insects, but females remain on the tree, removing, however, from the leaves to the twigs or branches.

The cut shows eggs as hatched in the spring.

REMEDIES.

This pest is so readily detected during the month of May, that wherever trees are infested they will be noticed at once, and where they were not destroyed last season, the trees or bushes should be sprayed or thoroughl washed during winter with solution No. 2 or No. 3.

There is a species of black ant that destroys the egg sac, and on that account it does not increase as do some of the other insect pests.

CURRANT FLY.

This insect has not yet, as known by this Board, visited the gardens of this province, but has been found in the neighboring state. Hence we deem t important to be on the watch for it, with the proper remedies for its extermination.

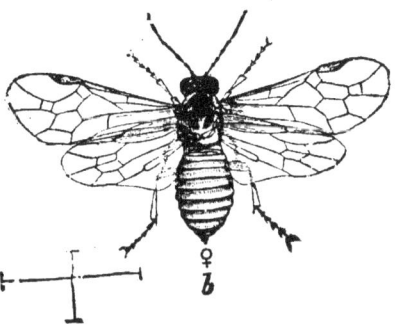

The perfect female is shown in the figure above, the lines showing the actual size.

This insect will ruin the currant and gooseberry crop, if once it has gained entrance and is allowed to go unmolested. In its perfect state it is a small two-winged fly which lays its eggs on the fruit while it is small. The larvæ enter the fruit yet green and feed on its contents, leaving a small black scar at point of entering. The affected fruit ripens prematurely and shortly decays and drops to the ground, when on opening them a small white grub will be found, about one-third of an inch long.

REMEDIES.

The following remedies have proved effectual where tried in other places: Use one large tablespoonful of powdered white hellebore dissolved in a pailful of water, spraying the bushes just before they bloom and again after the fruit has set.

Solution No. 1 is also recommended to be used at the time and in the manner mentioned for first remedy.

HOP PLANT LOUSE.

The Hop-louse has invaded the hop fields of Western Washington last eason more than any previous year, and it is now a question whether or not hop raising will take the same downward course as has been the case in Wisconsin and New York. In reference to the life history of this pest, Prof. Riley, U. S. Entomologist, who is authority, and to whose kindness we are indebted for the illustrations here given, writes as follows:

"Wherever it occurs, whether in England or on the continent of Europe, in New York, Wisconsin or on the Pacific coast, the Hop Plant Louse (*Phorodon humuli*) has substantially the same life-round. The eggs are laid in the fall on different varieties and species of the plum, both wild and cultivated. They are small, glossy, black, ovoid, and are attached to the terminal twigs, especially in the more or less protected crevices around the buds (Fig A).

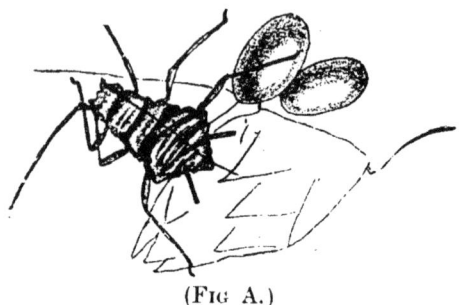

(FIG A.)

Winter egg of the Hop Plant Louse and shrivelled skin of the sexual female which laid them—enlarged.

From an egg hatches in the spring, about the time when the plum buds begin to burst, a stout female plant louse, known as the stem-mother, which differs from the summer individuals, by having shorter legs and shorter honey tubes.

She gives birth, without the intervention of the male, to living young, and this method of propogation continues until the last generation of the season. The second generation grows to full size and gives birth to a third, which becomes winged (Fig B), and develops after the hops have made considerable growth in the yards. The winged lice then fly from the plums to the hops, deserting the plum tree entirely and settling upon the leaves of the hops, where they begin giving birth to another generation of wingless individuals. These multiply with astonishing rapidity. Each female is capable of producing on an average about one hundred young, at the rate of three per day, under favorable conditions. Each generation begins to breed about the eighth day after birth, so that the issue from a single individual runs up, in the course of a summer, to trillions. The issue from a single stem-mother may thus, under favorable circumstances, blight hundreds of acres in the course of two or three months. From five to twelve generations are produced in the course of the summer, carrying us in point of time to the hop-picking season. There then develops a generation of winged females (sexuparæ), which fly back to the plum tree and give birth to the true sexual females (Fig. C),

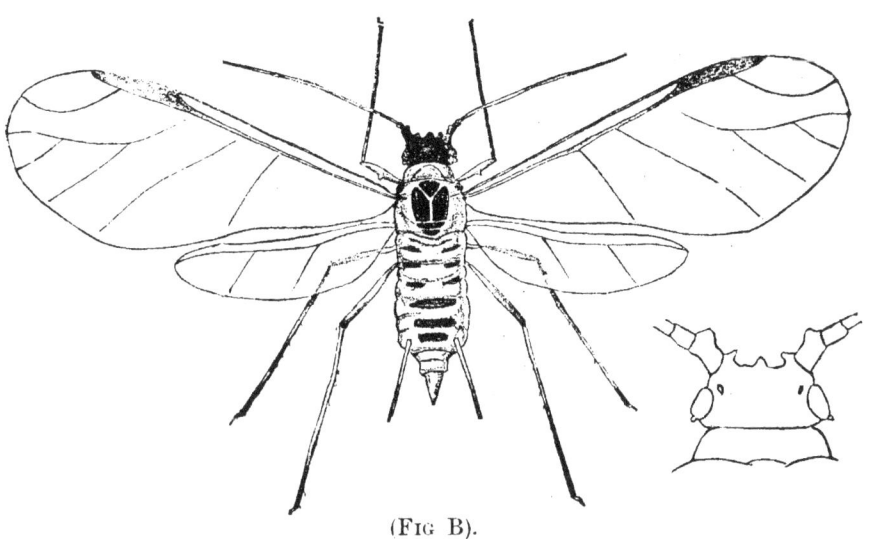

(FIG B).

The Hop Plant Louse, third generation on plum—the generation which flies to the hop. Head below at right. Both enlarged.

which never acquire wings and never leave the plum tree. By the time this generation has matured, which requires but a few days, varying according to the temperature, belated winged individuals which are the true males (Fig. D.) **fly** in from the hop fields. These fertilize the wingless true females upon

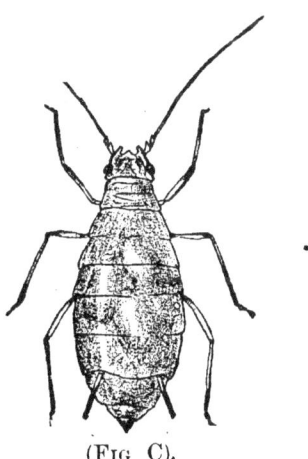

(FIG C).

The Hop Plant Louse, true sexual female— enlarged.

the plum leaves, and these soon thereafter lay the winter eggs. Thus, there is but one generation of sexed individuals produced, and this at the close of the life-round—the females wingless on plum trees; the males winged on hops. All intervening generations are composed of virgin females only (parthenagenetic). This is the invariable round of the insect's life.

REMEDIES.

From the life history just given, three important facts are obtained : (1) It will pay to make a preventive application of some of the mixtures mentioned further on, with apparatus before described, to all plum trees in the neighborhood of hop yards, either in the spring, before the appearance of the first winged generation and its consequent migration to hop, or in the fall after hop picking and after the lice have once more returned to the plum, and are making their preparations for the laying of winter eggs. The latter time will, perhaps, be preferable; for the reason that in the fall the plum trees will be less susceptible to the action of the washes, and a stronger solution can be applied without danger to the trees. (2) All wild plum trees in the woods through a hop-growing country should be destroyed. (3) The hop vines should be either burned or thoroughly drenched with kerosene emulsion as soon after the crop is harvested as possible, with a view of killing the males, and thus preventing the impregnation of the females. (4) If the above

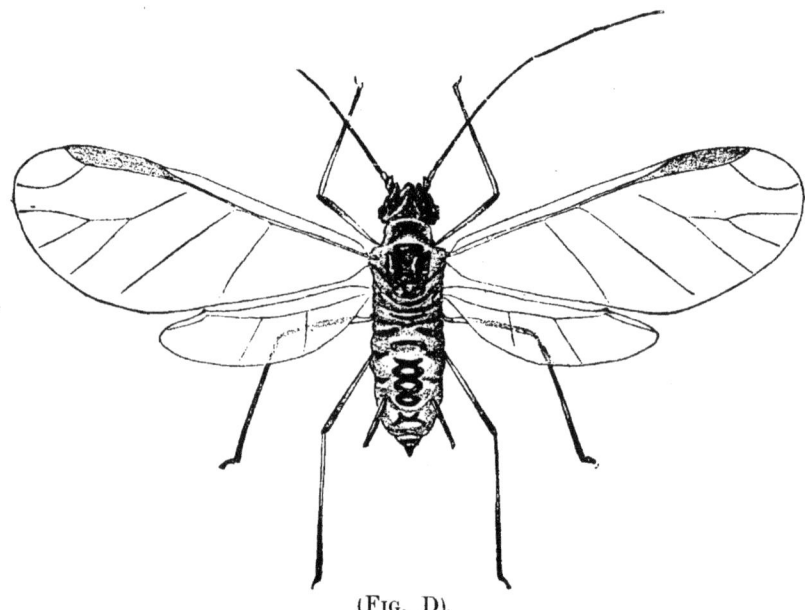

(FIG. D).

The Hop-Plant Louse, male—enlarged.

measures have been neglected and the lice have attacked the vines, the crop can still be protected by spraying with insecticide mixtures, which, if thoroughly applied, will prove effective, and there will be no danger of reinfestation from neighboring untreated yards, since during the summer the lice cannot migrate except by crawling from one yard to another.

SUBSTANCES TO BE USED.

Of all the different substances experimented with in 1888, none gave more satisfaction than properly prepared kerosene emulsions and fish oil soaps.

FORMULA FOR KEROSENE EMULSION.

Cheap kerosene..................................pints 8
Water... "   4
Soap...pounds ½

Dissolve the soap in the water and add, boiling hot, to the kerosene. Churn the mixture by means of a force pump and spray nozzle for five or ten minutes. The emulsion, if perfect, forms a cream which thickens on cooling, and should adhere without oiliness to the surface of glass. Dilute one part of the emulsion with twenty-five parts of water. A common grade of kerosene, which is good enough for this work, can be bought in most localities at eight cents per gallon by the barrel, and the soap used can be made for one cent per pound. This would make the batch given above cost eight and one-half cents, and diluted with twenty-five gallons of water to one of the emulsion would make thirty-eight and one-half gallons of wash. At this rate one hundred gallons would cost twenty cents.

FORMULA FOR TWENTY-FIVE POUNDS FISH-OIL SOAP.

Crystal potash lye ....pounds 1
Fish-oil......................................pints 2
Soft water....................................gallons 3

A strong suds made at the rate of one pound of this soap to eight gallons of water will also be found a uniformly safe and satisfactory wash to use, killing the lice and not harming the vines. After standing three days, however, the suds will lose its efficacy.

The Board also recommends the Quassia Chips solution which has been used with great efficiency in the hop yards of the Puyallup valley. Formula as follows:

QUASSIA CHIPS SOLUTION.

8 pounds of Quassia Chips.
7   "   " Whale-oil soap.

The quassia chips are boiled in about one gallon of water to each pound of chips, for one hour. The soap is added while hot, and allowed to dissolve. This solution is then diluted with 100 gallons of water. Use with sprayer.

TOMATO BLIGHT—GENERAL CAUSES AND REMEDY.

This disease of the tomato has made its appearance in the eastern part of the state, to such an extent in some localities as to cause growers to cease cultivating the tomato, which is a loss of many thousands of dollars to the state, as tomato growing for the markets is an important industry. The disease makes its appearance while the tomato is making its most vigorous growth during the month of July. The first sign of it is noticed by the leaves of the top of the plant beginning to turn yellow, this discoloration extending toward the roots until the plant perishes.

It has been discovered that plants which grow somewhat under a shade are not effected with the blight, and that such plants produce fine tomatoes. The Board suggests, by way of an experiment, that a light shade be placed on the south and southwest of each hill of tomatoes during the months of July and August. This can be done by placing two sticks in the ground, and stretch a piece of muslin over and tacking it to them. To preserve the muslin it could be painted with white lead or linseed oil. There have been many experiments made to discover the cause of blight to plant-life. Some scientists claim it originates from the work of a parasite ; that bacteria is found in the sap of limbs that are affected with blight. But the most reasonable conclusion reached by the leading scientists of the country, is that blight originates from such causes as frost, sun-scald and such influences which have the effect of changing the normal condition of the sap of the plant, thus causing an inter- ruption and stagnation of the sap. The sap is thus in a condition for bacteria to enter it. It then becomes a virus which is slowly carried through the tissues of the plant, and finally effects its death. A healthful tree inoculated with sap from a blighted plant will soon be discovered to have the blight. But limbs of a blighted tree placed in contact with a healthful tree will not affect the latter tree; it can only be accomplished by injecting affected material into the sap. The reason that a whole orchard will soon be affected is because the whole orchard has been subject to the same general cause as that of the first tree or plant, some local condition might prove favorable to one tree and not to another, as in the condition of the shaded tomato plant which did not blight.

The Board recommends that seed grown in Ohio, Kentucky, Tennessee and such states where tomato blight does not occur, be tried ; that seed grown places where tomato blight occurs should never be planted, as seed from such plants, although apparently healthy, have, nevertheless, in some degrees inherited the tendency to blight. The remedy usually recommended for blight is to cut away the affected part far below where affected, and see that the knife used is not used afterward upon healthy plants or trees without being thoroughly cleansed.

CABBAGE WORM.

(Pieris raphœ).

This worm, produced from the eggs of the white Rape Butterfly, is a most injurious pest to cabbage in most places, and especially in small gardens. They come in two broods, the first butterflies being seen in May, the second in August, and the progeny of the latter causes the most trouble. Either the same, or a else a very similar worm, also devours the Mignonette and some other plants.

PYRETHRUM OR BUHACH—LIQUID FORM.

A tablespoonful of the pure powder to two gallons of watre, applying it by sprinkling with a watering pot, or better yet, by force with a pump. Here, as in all cases where we use liquids to destroy insects, especially if, as in this case, it kills by contact, we must apply with great force, so that the liquid will spatter everywhere and so touch every insect.

CURRANT AND GOOSEBERRY SLUG OR WORM.

(Nematus ventricosus).

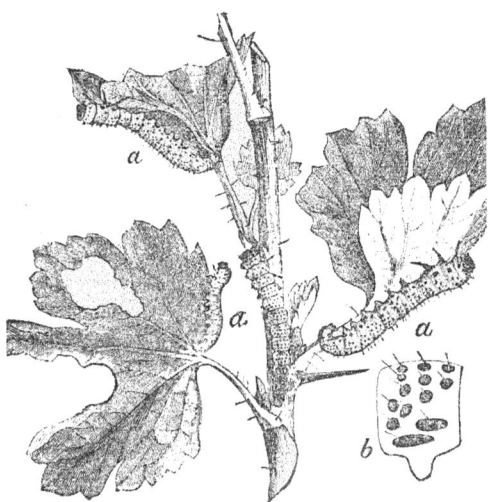

The full-grown worms are about three-fourths of an inch long, and are shewn at (a); (b) gives the position of the black spots upon a magnified joint of the body.

This voracious insect differs from the Cherry Slug. The flies are yellow, not black. The slugs are green, or green dotted with black, and not brown. They feed on the gooseberry or currant, and eat the leaf entire, instead of merely removing the cuticle. It is so readily dealt with by the timely application of remedies, that there can be no possible excuse for the shocking damage often seen done to these useful fruits about town and country homes.

POWDERED HELLEBORE.

Hellebore is the best of known remedies, and a perfectly effectual one. Properly applied, no harm can possibly result from it. It should, according to Prof. Lintner, be used in the following manner: Early in the spring, as soon as the leaves of the currant have fully put forth, watch for the first indications of the hatching and commencement of the young larvæ. You have only to look for these on the *lowest leaves of the bushes near the ground.* The indications will be numerous *small holes eaten into the leaves.* Sprinkle powdered hellebore over these leaves, renewing it if washed away by rain, and the desired end is accomplished. If the hellebore remains upon the leaves during the time that larvæ are hatching, all will be killed, and none will remain for subsequent spreading over the leaves and for the need of future attention. If the first brood of worms is thus destroyed, there will be few, if any, to form a second brood in June.

HAND PINCHING.

Some find it convenient to watch for the first eaten leaves, and to pinch them off by hand and destroy them. The eggs are always to be found conspicuously arranged in rows upon the veins of the under side of the leaves.

NICOTIN.

Laying some refuse tobacco stems from the cigarmakers', in the centre of each bush about May 1st, or mulching the bushes with tobacco stems, or these mixed with strawy manure, afford a complete remedy.

DUSTING WITH SOOT.

This has recently been recommended as being equally as destructive to this worm as is hellebore.

CUT WORMS.

(Agrotis, Noctuidæ, etc.).

Of these destructive worms, which have the habit of leaving their places of concealment in the soil, at night coming to the surface and cutting off almost every kind of newly set vegetable and flowering plants, there are now known to be many species. Those of the genus *Agrotis*, being mostly thick, greasy-looking caterpillars of some shade of gray, brown or green, variously marked, are the best known and well to be looked upon with dread.

(FIG. B.)

(FIG. A.)

These troublesome pests, which are doubtless the cause of more loss to farmers in the spring months than any other insects, are the caterpillars of a number of different dull-colored moths (Fig. A.) which fly at night. The worms, one kind of which is shown at Fig. B., are smooth, greasy-looking dark caterpillars, ranging from about ½ an inch to 2 inches in length at the time they injure crops. They feed at night and hide during the day time. The eggs of most species are laid in autumn, and the young caterpillars make about a quarter of their growth before winter sets in. They pass the winter in a torpid condition, and are ready in spring to attack the young crops as soon as they come up. The full growth of most species is completed by the first week in July, when the caterpillar forms a cell in the earth and changes to a chrysalis, from which the moth appears about a month later.

REMEDIES—CLEAN CULTURE.

As the young caterpillars of many species hatch in autumn, the removal of all vegetation from the ground as soon as possible in autumn deprives them of their food supply and also prevents the late-flying moths from laying their eggs in that locality. Fields or gardens which are allowed to become over-grown with weeds or other vegetation late in the autumn are almost sure to be troubled with cut worms the next spring.

BANDING AND WRAPPING.

It will be found to well repay the trouble and expense to place a band of tin around each cabbage or other plant at the same time of setting out. These may very easily be made by taking pieces of tin 6 inches long and 2½ wide and bending them around a spade or broom handle so as to form short tubes. In placing them around a plant the two ends can be sprung apart to admit the plant, and then the tube should be pressed about half an inch into the ground. I have found this a useful means of disposing of empty tomato and other cans. To prepare these easily, they need only be thrown into a bonfire, when the tops and bottoms fall off and the sides become unsoldered. The central piece of tin can then be cut down the centre with a pair of shears, and forms two tubes.

Wrapping a piece of paper round the stems of plants when setting them out will also save a great many.

POISONING.

Put a teaspoonful of Paris green or London purple in two gallons of water and sprinkle handfuls of grass, green sods or other vegetation, which can then be scattered throughout the patch, walking crossways of the harrow marks. By doing this towards evening after the last harrowing, during the night the cut worms that are deprived of their food will be out looking for fresh pastures, and will appropriate of the prepared bait, the smallest particle of the poison of which will kill. If the worms are very troublesome, the remedy can be repeated, it being easily applied.

SHIELDING THE STEM.

By encircling each plant that is set with a bit of tar paper, or even other paper, the ravages of the worm may be prevented. The paper should extend upwards several inches from a point just beneath the surface of the soil.

HUNTING AND KILLING.

By closely examining the surface of the soil in the morning, in the vicinity of their spoils, through dropping plants or otherwise their place of retreat may usually be discovered, and the worms killed.

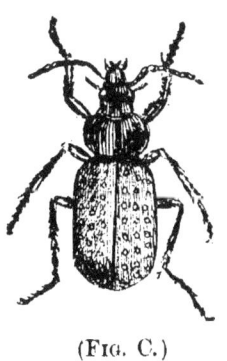

(Fig. C.)

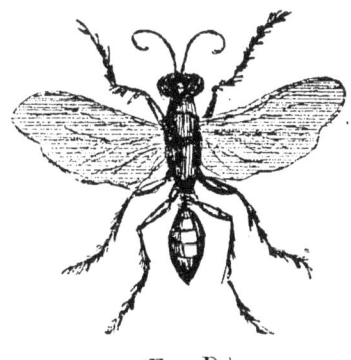

(Fig. D.)

NATURAL ENEMIES.

There are two enemies which deserve especial notice, and, from the good service they do, should be known by sight to every cultivator. They are the Fiery Ground-beetle or Cut Worm Lion *(Calosoma calidum*, Fab.)—Fig. C.— and the Black Ground Wasp *(Ammophila luctuosa)*—Fig. D). Both of these are desperate enemies of cut worms, the former feeding on them in all of its stages, the latter digging them out and storing its nest with them as food for its young grubs.

Remedies, as quoted elsewhere.

D. M. Jessee. of Walla Walla, Wash., who has been elected state fruit pest inspector by the Board of Horticulture, gives the following remedy which has proven by experience to be effectual in destroying all insects and fruit pests thus far known. This will hereafter be known as

"SOLUTION NO. 1."—USE WITH SPRAY PUMP.

For summer spraying: Take two gallons of water; put into this one pound sulphur, one pound concentrated lye; boil for two hours, then add one half gallon fish oil; boil until it makes a hard soap; add one half gallon kerosene oil, stir well and boil a few minutes. Add to this twenty-five gallons cold water. For winter spraying double all the ingredients for the amount of water used.

This solution, with a sprayer, will be effective in destroying the Aphis.

SOLUTION NO. 2.

Three pounds soap (whaleoil or good home-made soap), three lbs. sulphur, one can lye; boil one hour in four gallons water; add one gallon kerosene oil; boil slow twenty minutes, then add twenty-five gallons water; use with spray pump. Do not use copper kettle in preparing solution No. 1 and No. 2. but use kettle made of iron or some other metal.

SOLUTION NO. 3.

One pound of concentrated lye to five gallons of water; apply warm with spray pump: or six pounds of blue vitrol to twenty-five gallons of water.

SOLUTION NO. 4.—SAL SODA AND LYE.

This effectual remedy has been recommended by horticultural officials of other states, but some difficulty is found in keeping the right temperature while using it. "Two pounds of rosin; three pounds of sal soda, or one of concentrated lye; water to make thirty-six pints. Dissolve the sal soda or lye in a few pints of water. When thoroughly dissolved add the rosin. Heat until dissolved, and add water finally. Use one and one-half pints of the solution to the gallon of water. Use at a temperature of one hundred degrees Fahrenheit."

SOLUTION NO. 5.—WHALE OIL SOAP AND KEROSENE.

The following formula is from the Department of Agriculture, Washington: "Take two pounds of common or whale oil soap; one gallon water. Heat this solution and add it. boiling hot, to two gallons kerosene oil; churn this mixture by means of a force pump for ten minutes. The emulsion, if perfect, forms a cream, which thickens on cooling, and should adhere without oiliness to the surface of glass. Dilute before using, one part of the emulsion to nine parts of cold water."

SOLUTION NO. 6.—TOBACCO AND SOAP.

"Take five pounds of leaf tobacco and boil it from two to three hours in twenty gallons of water. Take one gallon of common soft soap and boil it in ten gallons of water until thoroughly mixed ; add the two together and strain."

Apply any of these mixtures by means of a spray pump as soon as the eggs begin to hatch, and continue the treatment as long as there is one Aphis to be found.

SOLUTION NO. 7.—LYE AND ROSIN.

The following is also recommended for winter wash ; One pound of concentrated lye (American or Babbitt's) ; one-half pound of rosin ; two and one-half gallons of water.

First dissolve the lye in water, and when thoroughly dissolved by heating, add the rosin ; use at a temperature of 100 degrees Fahrenheit.

For use when the tree is in foliage, dilute by using ten times the quantity of water. The summer wash is attended with best results when applied when a majority of the insects are hatched out. The first brood generally appears when the cherries are turning color. Badly infested trees should be treated to several applications of the wash with an interval of ten days.

Apply these mixtures by means of spray pumps.

KEROSENE EMULSION.

Professor Forbes has recommended that the roots of nursery trees be "puddled" with the kerosene emulsion before sending out, and that if the lice are seen upon the trunks, these be also treated with the emulsion, applying with a brush, sponge or cloth.

REMEDY FOR APPLE SCAB.—HOME MANUFACTURE OF COPPER CARBONATE.

"As the precipitated form of carbonate of copper is not always obtainable from druggists, directions are herewith appended for the easy preparation of this material at a cost much less than the usual wholesale price.

"In a vessel capable of holding two or three gallons, dissolve $1\frac{1}{2}$ pounds of copper sulphate (blue vitriol) in two quarts of hot water. This will be entirely dissolved in fifteen or twenty minutes, using the crystalline form. In another vessel dissolve $1\frac{3}{4}$ pounds of sal soda (washing soda) also in 2 quarts of hot water. When completely dissolved, pour the second solution into the first, stirring briskly. When effervescence has ceased, fill the vessel with water and stir thoroughly ; then allow it to stand five or six hours, when the sediment will have settled to the bottom. Pour off the clear liquid without disturbing the precipitate, fill with water again and stir as before, then allow it to stand until the sediment has settled again, which will take place in a few hours. Pour the clear liquid off carefully as before, and the residue is *carbonate of copper*. Using the above quantities of copper sulphate and sal soda, there will be formed 12 ounces of copper carbonate.

"Instead of drying this, which is a tedious operation, add four quarts of strong ammonia, stirring in well, then add sufficient water to bring the whole quantity up to 6 quarts. This can be kept in an ordinary two gallon stone jar, which should be closely corked.

FORMULA.

"Each quart will contain 2 ounces of the carbonate of copper, which, when added to 25 gallons of water, will furnish a solution for spraying, of the same strength and character as that obtained by the use of dried carbonate, and one which can be prepared with little labor, and kept ready for use throughout the season.

CARBONATE OF COPPER IN SUSPENSION.

"When the carbonate is to be used in suspension, instead of adding the ammonia to the sediment, add water until the whole quantity is made up to 6 quarts. Stir this thoroughly until the sediment is completely suspended (entirely mixed throughout) and pour the thick liquid into a suitable jar, when it will be ready for use.

"Before using shake the contents thoroughly, so that all the sediment may be evenly distributed in the water. Pour out a quart of the thick fluid and mix with 25 gallons of water.

"Horticulturist Experimental Farms.   JOHN CRAIG."

Professor Maynard, of Massachusetts Agricultural College, sums up the following as facts now pretty well settled, viz :

(1) That of the arsenites, Paris green gives the best results as an insecti-side.

(2) That the longer the mixture containing the arsenites stands, the greater the injury from soluble arsenic.

(3) That the foliage of the peach, plum and cherry is more susceptible to injury than that of the apple and pear.

(4) That the injury varies with the varieties, some being more susceptible than others.

(5) That young leaves are less injured than those fully developed, and are more injured on weak trees than on those that are vigorous and healthy.

(6) That Paris green cannot be used alone with safety, stronger than one pound to three hundred gallons of water, but with the lime mixtures it may be safely used at one pound to from fifty to two hundred gallons.

(7) That the foliage is most injured when kept constantly wet by light rains or foggy weather, but that heavy rains lessen the injury.

(8) That the least injury is done when the liquid dries off most rapidly.

(9) That the time of day when the application is made is unimportant.

CPSIA information can be obtained
at www.ICGtesting.com
Printed in the USA
BVHW04*1353210918
528174BV00011B/473/P

9 780484 599283